Relentless Healing

RELENTLESS HEALING

Your Practical Guide for Healing Based on God's Promises

Nicole Marie Aldridge, MS, CCC-SLP

YouSpeakIt
PUBLISHING
*The Easy Way
to Get Your Book
Done Right*™

To my husband, my rock and love of my life, Jon.
Thank you for your relentless support, love, joy, and grace.

Contents

Acknowledgments   9

Introduction   11

CHAPTER ONE

God's Promise Of Healing   17

     Jesus Heals   17

     The Holy Spirit   25

     God Is Alive   34

CHAPTER TWO

Feel Like You've Tried It All?   47

     You're Not Done Yet   47

     Your Mind Leads; Your Body Follows   55

     Willing To Be Sculpted   64

CHAPTER THREE

Navigating The Healthcare System   75

     The Role Of Health Insurance   75

     God Uses Many Hands   83

     The Reality Of Payment   91

CHAPTER FOUR

How To Discern God's Lead—

     A Practical Application   97

     Gut Feelings   97

     Learning As You Go   106

     Processes   113

CHAPTER FIVE

Encouraging And Empowering:
How To Use This Framework   125
    Commitment   125
    Giving Yourself Grace   135
    Forming New Habits   143

Conclusion   149
Next Steps   153
About the Author   155

Acknowledgments

I'm thankful for God and the people He led me to.

To name some in particular: My loving and inspiring husband, Jon.

My family: Bob and Kathy, Philip and Fallon, Grandma and Pakey, Grandma Jones, Aunt Linda and Uncle Joe, Uncle Bobby and Aunt Nancy, Ang, Will, and Annabeth, Nick and Sylwia and the boys, the Griffeths, Jess, Liana, Asher and Luca, Jules, Aunt Dot, Uncle Steve and Aunt Rebecca, Sue and Bruce, Peter, Lyn, Brian, Mary, and Doug.

My dear friends: Abby, Jess, Vivienne, Marissa and Jeremy, Mara, Issy, Julia, Courtney, Emily, Shauna, Liz Rooney, Cassandra, Peter, Abigail, Fran, Lori, and Starla.

Churches across the nation, especially All Nations Church in Newport News, Virginia, St. Lukes in North Carolina, Elevation Church in Raleigh, North Carolina, and Freedom Life Church in Viginia.

Dr. Caroline Leaf, Pastor Stephen Furtick, Kyle Cease, Martha Owens, Cindy Higgins, Brian Forrester, Dr. Durham, Sarah Martin, Sarah Ratti, Dr. Gregory O'Shanick, Madison Moore Brown, Dr. Liz Caughey, Mike Cantrell, Dr. Jeffery Brown, Jennifer Sujarna, and the YouSpeakIt Publishing and editing team.

Thank you all, and thanks also to all those God puts in my path in the coming days.

Introduction

Welcome. I'm so grateful our paths have crossed. I firmly believe that in this crossing, our lives will never be the same.

The Creator of the World loves each of us so intimately and powerfully that He gave His only son for us. As a result, we have many gifts available. In this book, I specifically focus on His gift of complete healing and how you can receive that in a variety of ways. I want you to relentlessly pursue the promise of healing. I share the many ways in which I was led to this promise, and I hope to offer the same opportunity to you.

Lord knows, I spent my greater adult life trying to understand and live out what would truly make me complete—to live a life I was excited about living. I absolutely had happiness in my life. I had a loving husband, a beautiful home, a successful career as a speech-language pathologist, and a great network of friends and family. I was involved in my church and community and believed in Christ as my savior.

I spent Monday through Friday helping others who had difficulty communicating, some with great neurological deficits. And while I enjoyed much of what I did and who I was in those acts, I had this nagging feeling that I was missing the point. I was missing the real depth, connection, and reason for life.

If this is it, God, I'm ready.

It wasn't until I was falling to the earth, headfirst, with nothing but boulders below that I truly understood what was important in life. On April 12, 2014, I fell while bouldering in Red Rocks State Park in Las Vegas, Nevada. I was a significant distance above my husband, who was just beyond a catchable distance. My hands were pinned between my body and the boulder I was climbing as I fell headfirst toward a ravine of boulders below.

I realized that I was about to hit boulders with my head and neck. Given my education as a speech-language pathologist, I had a basic understanding of anatomy and neurological function. I knew the wide array of results that might ensue, including the possibility of death. My simple prayer was: *If this is it, God, I'm ready.*

It suddenly became so clear. That's what life's about: connection with our Creator in all things, and not just any kind of connection. A deep, loving connection that is all encompassing.

In those fleeting moments before hitting the ground, my life came before my eyes—like a flip book in my mind's eye— and everything of this world paled in comparison to this clarity. Everything. The fights with my husband, my place of employment, the type of clothing I wore, or the food I ate. All of it was drowned out in this giant wave of loving connection with God.

My life journey took a turn that day. I ricocheted between boulders, head and neck taking the blow, and was ultimately wedged between two rocks. I was carried out of the desert, in and out of consciousness, to the hospital.

I eventually came to learn I had suffered a concussion, not to mention that I had split my forehead open in a couple places, had suffered whiplash, and had developed a kind of vertigo called *benign paroxysmal positional vertigo* (BPPV), caused by crystals in my cochlea being dislodged The concussion was my fourth in my early young adulthood and ultimately led to a traumatic brain injury (TBI).

I was chronically dizzy, to the point that I couldn't get out of bed. I was constantly nauseous with loss of taste. Everything looked double and speckled. My depth perception made everything look like a picture in a magazine, and my scope of vision was so impacted that I wasn't able to see in more than a one-foot radius around my face.

I couldn't track text with my eyes, so I could no longer read. Light and sound sensitivity was so amped up that the dog barking or sunlight shining into the window resulted in instant migraines, heart palpitations, and flashes of light. My hands and feet were always cold and would often go numb, and I would be exhausted after being awake for a mere five hours.

My quality of life suffered immensely. I could no longer take part in basic tasks around the house, let alone things

I enjoyed. My relationships suffered and I became angry and bitter. While I tried to work, I ultimately lost my job. Misunderstood and depressed, I began to deeply wonder why I didn't die that day. And while I'd love to say that I was given a grand realization that gave me clarity and passion for ultimate healing in the name of Jesus, this didn't happen.

To be honest, I still sometimes find myself in seasons of deep struggle. But ultimately, I come back to the truth I received on April 12, 2014: *It's all about a loving, deep connection with my Heavenly Father.*

Thus began my pursuit of health and healing. As I write this book, over four years later, I am humbly grateful for all God has accomplished in me through this event. I continue to pursue the coming forth of His healing in my body and have become unshakably passionate about sharing and guiding others on their healing journeys.

This path is of grand design, and I hope my story will be an example of the goodness that can be birthed from a tumultuous season. I want to offer you peace, guidance, and understanding as you forge the path before you.

What's in store:

This handbook is meant to guide you in receiving healing in whatever way possible, including receiving the best care through the healthcare system. In order to survive this process, you must have faith—in yourself, in the promise of healing, in God, in the universe. We are going to start off talking *big* so we can gain a clear idea of what and where we are in this design. Even when life swings like crazy, these universal truths never ever change. We will come back to these throughout our discussion.

As you delve into this, be sure to do so with intention. Set yourself up for success so you are able to fully absorb how God is speaking to you through the text. Take notes. Circle and highlight, as there may be passages you'd like to read again. Be cognizant of how you are being led to read the text. You may find that reading it from page one forward is how it flows for you, but if you are feeling led in other ways, then I encourage you to follow that tug and read as you are led.

I hope you receive a deeper relationship with our Creator and that complete healing comes forth in your body, mind, and soul in Jesus's name.

CHAPTER ONE

_____

God's Promise of Healing

JESUS HEALS

I was going to blow them away so that I could declare complete healing in the name of Jesus. Sounds great, doesn't it?

So, I followed all the medical advice, continued working full time, kept up with all household tasks, and still went out with friends and family as if nothing was different. I wasn't told to do otherwise—at least not by human beings. I followed the protocols the medical community gave me—with textbook application—for one year. Physical therapy, rest as I felt I needed it, medication and herbals as prescribed, a change in my contacts prescription, and dietary changes. However, I was not getting better; I was, in fact, getting worse.

Over time, I began to notice my body communicating to me in ways people couldn't. I didn't understand what it was saying for many months. As I moved forward, pursuing the road I had set my mind to, my health and function began to suffer. This mentality of overcoming sickness by following protocols and living my life unencumbered soon became a roadblock to my healing journey. I came to see I was taking part in activities despite the messages my body was giving me.

My focus until this point had been on the injury and resisting the symptoms. Like they were roadblocks in my path before me, I was bound and determined to overcome these symptoms—rooted in spite.

I had accepted Jesus into my life years prior, but one day I had a moment in which I recognized the need to do something differently.

I had just passed the one-year anniversary of my injury, and I was hanging on by a thread. At this point, basic, simple tasks of life were now extremely challenging, and I was completely unable to do many of them. I slept, performed my basic tasks at work, and then went back to bed.

A grocery store felt like a warzone when I walked in. Thinking about how to prepare a meal was like asking my brain to complete calculus. Driving for more than fifteen minutes led to migraines.

How could this be?

I followed all the medical professionals' recommendations. I ate right and was sure as hell sleeping enough. I believed in my healing.

Or did I?

I had faith and went to church. But maybe there was something more, something critical I was missing.

One day, I came home from work, feeling like a shell of a person. I felt thin, like the skin freshly shed from a snake—a ghostly form of what I once encased. Tired, nauseous, and with a roaring headache, I sat down at our pedestal table and dropped my head in my hands.

Something needed to change.

I felt a strong pull that I needed to let God use this. Not just this moment. This whole thing. My whole life. That moment is what opened my understanding to the realness of what Jesus did for us.

Jesus Healed Them All

> *Jesus traveled throughout the region of Galilee,*
> *teaching in the synagogues and announcing the*
> *Good News about the Kingdom. He healed every*
> *kind of disease and illness.*
>   Matthew 4:23, NLT

God's promise of healing through the acts of Jesus Christ is written in forty-one places in scripture. As I studied these scriptures, I came to see a consistent pattern: healing freely given to *all*. In reality, no one is excluded. In fact, Jesus did miraculous things for people others thought beyond help.

This really hit home for me. When God revealed this, the medical professionals working with me were beginning to say they had done all they could do for me. Increasingly, I was hearing about coping strategies on how to live with my injury. The reality that *Jesus healed them all* provided a conduit for me to pursue the path before me and to faithfully know and trust this was a promise for me as well. It is also a promise for you and each and every other child of His.

To go deeper, I encourage you to look in the back of the Bible under "God's Promises" to know what He promises in scripture.

Jesus Makes His Home In and Among Those Who Love Him

> *On that day, you will realize that I am in my Father, and you are in me, and I am in you.*
> John 14:20, NIV

This is my favorite verse. It encapsulates what Jesus has done for us and provides the real access we have to our Creator and to Jesus through the Holy Spirit. That access is gifted to each of us freely, thanks to Jesus. Through the Holy Spirit, Jesus tells us that he is housed within our hearts.

Maybe this is a stretch—but are you willing to take a dive with me?

To me, if Jesus is telling us here that he is in the Father—that he and the creator of the universe are one—and God and Jesus are one and *we are in* Jesus—that tells me that we are gifted with a covering of redemption and power, peace, and mercy that is rooted in the Holy Trinity. And not only that—but that it also lives in us. Why is that important? This means that you are so loved and important that, by God's design, He is already within your heart and enveloping your life. So, no matter what this world may throw your way, God, and all that He is, is available to you.

He also has such rich and beautiful everlasting gifts to give us, gifts that make the treasures of this world pale in comparison. Let's take healing as an example. If I had arthritis, for instance, this world might recommend medication to numb the symptoms.

But God can say: *There's healing already in this child of mine because I AM. I AM in them. And I AM able. I AM perfect design and this body is my Holy Temple. I long for complete healing in all that is housed in this body.*

God has the ability to bring forth that healing by his design. He will lead that temple of his into perfect and complete healing whether it is through prayer, therapy, diet modifications, or other methods. You are the hands and feet of Jesus now, and you are designed to live in his image. Living in his image helps us discern and pursue the abundant life that God has designed for us.

I think about the power of God and all that Jesus did and realize this power is something we can plug in to; we should not take this reality lightly. It took me a lot of time, study, and guidance from God to really understand it, but I encourage you to do the same. A simple search on YouTube for sermon series based on complete healing is one place to start.

This access is there and real and very personal. It provides a powerful avenue to connect with our savior in all aspects of our lives. That access is gifted to each of us freely, thanks to Jesus.

What He Took on the Cross

> *He personally carried our sins in His body on the cross so that we could be dead to sin and live for what is right. By His wounds, you are healed.*
> I Peter 2:24, NLT

By His wounds, you are healed. As believers in Christ and children of God, we have the gift of complete healing in our bodies and minds. Christ took all sickness, illness, ailment, injury, virus, and disease to the cross where their power died and was buried forever.

While I believed in this deeply, looking back, I seriously struggled to live it. I didn't realize it but I found myself walking in sickness, defined in each moment of my life by activities I couldn't do or ways I needed to adjust my life in order to cope—to cope with my symptoms in order to function. It is so obvious to me now, but at the time, I couldn't see how that was living in sickness. So, prayer and professing that this was all in Christ's hands was great, but at this season I was really struggling to let go and to discern how God wanted to set me free from the symptoms altogether.

I didn't fully receive the understanding, on a personal level, that Jesus Christ took all sickness, disease, injury, or ailment on the cross so that we didn't have to until I was given this opportunity to apply it. God led me to a powerful personal experience in which I underwent miraculous healing in a quiet setting.

At this time, my symptoms were limiting my ability to drive, work, and connect with others. I couldn't talk on the phone for long periods of time or take part in thought-provoking conversation due to brain fog and fatigue. I was oversensitive to lights and sounds, so I could no longer listen to music in the car nor go out at night because both resulted in instant migraines.

I had a headache all day, every day. I went to sleep with one, praying to be released from it come morning. But each morning, I would wake to a splitting headache. My nutrition was still quite poor due to continued headaches and nausea, and my fatigue was significant. I was no longer working, couldn't read one paragraph in a sitting, and could only walk about five houses down the street and back.

Two years post injury, I traveled to a small town in North Carolina to see a specialist for a two-week intensive program. During the weekend, I was led to St. Luke's church.

I say *led* because it was a tiny church nestled in the foothills on the outskirts of town. The only reason I knew of its existence was because my cabdriver mentioned it. I awoke Sunday morning with this intense pull to attend. The church seated about one hundred people. Simple whitewashed walls held wooden pews that lined the center aisle. It was an intimate group. The sermon was powerful and livened my soul.

Then, the pastor welcomed people forward for a laying on of hands for healing. While I had been in churches that practiced healing prayer, this time my spirit knew deep within—a visceral knowing—that I needed to go forward. I did and was shaking from head to toe. When the pastor put her hands on me, it was an out-of-this-world experience. Words don't really do it justice.

I felt energy travel through me. My eyes were closed, and I saw brilliant white light and an image of the cross. I could hear her speaking over me and could feel fellow church members lay hands upon me. We had intense prayer, and afterward, I was unable to move. I stayed in prayer, overwhelmed and grateful for such a miraculous gift.

I was powerfully changed. In complete awe. I remember one church member exclaiming, "She's just received the Holy Spirit!" I know in my heart that I connected with it completely. I walked out of that church symptom-free. At that time, my lifestyle was severely impacted by my injury, but I walked out of that church symptom-free. That experience was a window through which God showed me what the cross has done for all of us.

And as the days passed and some symptoms returned, I knew in my spirit that God gifted me that day with a window into what complete healing felt like. And it gave me experiential knowledge with which to move forward.

I came to know in my spirit that He is in it for me. He is also in it for you. I'm just one of the many. I'm grateful for the ability to be in a place now where I can spread that news to others.

THE HOLY SPIRIT

> *Do you not know that your bodies are temples of the Holy Spirit, who is in you, whom you have received from God? You are not your own.*
> 1 Corinthians 6:19, NIV

Each of us is made up of our spirit, our soul, and our body. Our body is comprised of the tissues, organs—including the brain—and physical being we all see and feel. Our spirit is the precious piece of us designed in God's perfect image that will be with Him for eternity. Our soul lives in a tenuous place between the two.

One critical thing our soul houses is our mind. An analogy I've heard often is this: If our brain were the computer, then our mind would be the software. The actual hardware of the computer is good at doing what it is told to do. The software tells it what to do. And, if we have the gift of the Holy Spirit as one with our spirit—living in and among our bodies—then God's design calls us to wrap our mind around the Holy Spirit's guidance in order to lead our bodies into alignment with scripture. Through this continuous renewed connection to the Holy Spirit, we have software running the computer in alignment with God's will.

For the longest time, I didn't understand what the Holy Spirit was. I grew up Catholic, and they talk about the Holy Ghost. I had this image of Casper being there all the time. In my young adulthood as a Christian, I kind of skipped this concept, and it was something not really in my focus. My focus was more about understanding God and understanding how Jesus was His son.

I came to recognize how palpable the presence of the Holy Spirit can be and how personal the Holy Spirit is. Through the knowledge and understanding of what we are about to delve into, I believe we are designed to live our life in constant connection to the Holy Spirit.

For example, when beginning prayer, I first claim the truth of 1 Corinthians 6:19. I began this section with these words: *Do you not know that your bodies are temples of the Holy Spirit?*

In all things, I cue this truth first, and I encourage you to explore doing the same as I believe this scripture reminds our minds of the software already downloaded onto our hard drive, so that our minds are then focused on God's design and able to run software that is connected to the Holy Trinity.

He Sent a Helper

> *Don't let your hearts be troubled. Trust in God,*
> *and trust also in me.*
>
> John 14:1, NLT

> *But in fact, it is best for you that I go away, because*
> *if I don't, the Advocate won't come. If I do go away,*
> *then I will send him to you.*
>
> John 16:7, NLT

Jesus is letting the disciples know he is about to be crucified. They're all upset about it. He is comforting them with this message: At this time, he was only flesh and accessible in a measured way. Once he went through this process, then the Holy Spirit provided what Jesus had been providing, but now, accessible to all and transcending all of time.

I experienced moments in which it was undeniable that God was at work. My understanding of the Holy Spirit grew. I was feeling it in my heart; I experienced a physical sensation at my heart center. Everyone recognizes the Holy Spirit is present in a unique way. At any rate, I started to recognize God was showing me the Holy Spirit. In moments when I was being challenged by my faith, He used it as a reminder. So in a way, there is this parallel of how the Holy Spirit is designed. The trials of life, the darkness, the valley—these all provide fertile soil for the connection with the Holy Spirit to be fostered.

The Holy Spirit is actually alive and accessible within each of us all the time. God's design was for us to utilize the Holy Spirit constantly. It is a powerful truth that the Creator of heaven and Earth, of the first molecule and blade of grass, of all that is seen and unseen—that part of His design for all humanity was to have constant access to His Holy Spirit.

He provides anything for us when we ask in the name of Jesus. (John 14:13) We have been given something deeply and profoundly exceptional that our Heavenly Father designed to be woven into our lives at a personal level. He is intimately involved and longs to be a part of our individual needs and decisions—how we live our life. He is interested in being a part of our personal life and is ready and able to provide us with guidance through the Holy Spirit.

As we continue to explore and welcome this truth into our lives, we can find ourselves growing spiritually. This truth is a conduit to finding what we are seeking at a spiritual level.

The journey can feel challenging. I encourage you to see this truth and trust that God will work in you just as He worked in me. I'm hopeful that this book will help by being one of those resources. My injury and resulting healing journey became a pressure cooker of sorts for spiritual growth. I grew very deep in my faith in a very short period of time.

Knowing God at a Personal Level

In being called to use, access, and connect with the Holy Spirit, we are given the ability to experience a greater relationship with God. In doing so, we achieve greater intimacy with Him. We go along for the ride, letting God do what He does. The key lies in the power of that connection and our need to be an active participant in connecting.

I have heard that when God gives us something, it's the parallel of being given a gift in this world. Imagine you receive a package. Maybe it's wrapped in shiny, crisp paper or delicate and dainty in elegant, textured giftwrap, all tied up in a big beautiful bow. Can you picture it?

Now imagine you let it sit there. You never pick it up, never open it.

What good is the gift if you're not opening it, if you're not actively using what you have been given?

The purpose of the gift was for you to receive it, open it, and enjoy it! Use what is within; use the gift. It's the same with the Holy Spirit in relation to healing. Once we gain access to what God is doing in our life and understand how to live it out, we can be most receptive.

Recognize you are committing to knowing God and knowing yourself. You are the only you there is, and this is the only life you have.

Go ahead and take this time. Find that opportunity in the day to recognize how the Holy Spirit is showing up for you. Notice the feelings in your body, colors you may see, images that arise, tastes or sounds working through your sensory system, and give yourself a bit of a daily challenge, realizing what comes with each physical sensation.

For knowing God is the way we are designed to function. Not just at church, or just in our deepest need, but in all things. In all parts of our life and in all times throughout our day. To know Him is to receive the Holy Spirit. And to receive the Holy Spirit is to utilize connection to the Holy Spirit in more and more of your thought life. And when your thought life is connected, utilizing this gift, the body follows, resulting in receiving the promises of scripture.

Living in Communion

Once we've recognized that the Holy Spirit is leading us and we commit to fostering the relationship with God personally, our practice is then to recognize how He's leading us. He is doing whatever He wants to do in our lives.

Maybe you are searching for forgiveness, acceptance, lifestyle adjustment, sleep hygiene, or other needs. Once you delve into this kind of practice, you are constructing an avenue to an open and constant connection with the gift living within you. This is living in communion.

When it comes to our health, well-being, and healing, lots of factors are at play, such as:

- Navigating the healthcare system
- Spiritual practices
- Lifestyle
- Tips and tools

Are you asking: *How do I navigate all of this?*

When I ask this question, I know I need to recalibrate my focus. Like a ship navigating the seas, I need to remember that I am in God's hands; and therefore, I need to go ahead and take time to access the Holy Spirit for clarification.

I recommend a simple practice:

1. Stop.

2. Breathe.

3. Come to your center.

4. Remember you are loved unconditionally and held in His hands forever by our heavenly Father's grace.

When exploring this access to the Holy Spirit, you must be completely honest. Recognize that God already knows all of you anyway.

Keep in mind this passage from Psalms:

> *You made all the delicate, inner parts of my body*
> *and knit me together in my mother's womb.*
> Psalm 139:13, NLT

It's between the two of you. It needs to be unfiltered and honest.

I participate in this recalibration—not because I need to find the answer, although that will often come—but because I recognize the need to reconnect with my savior in this arena. In this way, no matter how small or big the connection may seem, I am opening up and welcoming Him so I may receive the gift of the Advocate, Comforter, Holy Spirit. (John 14:26)

Then, He is in control and I am along for the ride. God wants it all. He tells us He is not interested in only parts of us and our lives. He is interested in being a part of all that this life has to offer. All of it. (Matthew 6:33, Romans 12:1)

I realized patterns were coming up as I journaled in drawings and different formats. I had to recognize with no judgment and in an open, honest way that something was at the forefront, coming up. For example, I used this connection for navigating the healthcare system. In my case, in order to live out a symptom-free, completely healed life, my body needed to pursue care from a variety of specialists.

After coming home one day feeling like a shell of a person, we decided I needed to put my health first. The next day, I put in a request for leave through FMLA (Family Medical Leave Act). I went out on medical leave.

You know this old cliché? *If you don't take care of you, you're not good to anybody.*

The career of a speech therapist is to give of self with each patient. But I had nothing left to give. We responded to the pull away from my career as it became apparent that it was inhibiting my gift of complete healing. We dedicated the rest of our resources to whatever we needed to do for my care. No constraints. Which meant having an open mind about going to clinics that did not accept insurance or out-of-network clinics and being open to nontraditional interventions, such as acupuncture, massage, hands-on prayer, vibrational patterns, and states of mind.

I delved into research of our neurological systems and how they may be impacted. I studied how to use that information as a tool to influence my neurological system for healing.

I felt immensely close to God and strong spiritually. I felt a renewed sense of clarity and discerned what I needed to do as my next step to receive healing. I knew of the gift of neuroplasticity and I was going to utilize it.

God led me to know and understand how to utilize in my life the biblical truths related to healing—that we are created in His image and are His children. He promises goodness and complete health and healing for each and every one of us. And sure enough, bit by bit, step by step, I was led to resources to help bring that healing forth in my body.

The Holy Spirit can feel abstract and a little messy. It is to some extent. At the same time, I believe we are designed to live in constant communion so we can live out our life in the fullness it was meant to be lived.

What better motivator is there?

GOD IS ALIVE

> *For the word of God is alive and powerful. It is sharper than the sharpest two-edged sword, cutting between soul and spirit, between joint and marrow. It exposes our innermost thoughts and desires.*
>
> Hebrews 4:12, NLT

I think it's easy to think of God as the big guy in the sky and someone we're going to meet after we take our last breath. Through my healing journey, God showed me that He is so much more. In fact, He is alive today and is interested in the whole you.

No Coincidences

Do you ever have those moments where you think: *What are the odds?*

It stops you for a minute to think about how that instance impacted your life in a unique and sometimes powerful way. I experienced these kinds of moments with extreme frequency shortly after these health challenges in my journey.

For example, during a physical therapy appointment one day, I got talking with a fellow patient around my age and ended up finding out that she, too, had suffered many head injuries. It was through my relationship with her that I learned of a clinic out of town that specialized in brain injury cases.

At one point, we didn't know how we were going to pay our bills, but God made a way for me financially. That very same day, we received an insurance reimbursement check in the mail for the exact same amount owed. That's God right there!

It was in my cab ride from my Airbnb to the clinic that I learned of a small church in town. While in the small church, I received a miracle.

What are the odds?

Our lives are forever changed because of these coincidental moments. Those moments are not unique to me or my family. The more I share about my coincidences, the more I hear others who relate or have their own story.

For those of us who are believers, we can see those moments as opportunities to say: *Is this more than what it appears to be on the surface?*

Often, we find those moments are God's way of moving in our lives. The Bible tells us that one way God is alive in our midst and on this Earth is that He works through others. To explore further, I encourage you to look at 2 Kings 5:1–14.

Here, God shares with us a story that is rich with discernment, active engagement in our pursuit of healing, and ultimate receiving of His healing promise.

It is the story of the healing of Naaman. In it, Naaman—described as a good and successful man—is in favor of the king of his land, Aram, who suffers from leprosy. An Isreali captive tells Naaman's wife of a charge she believes is critical for Naaman: *Go to the land of Samaria, visit a prophet who will heal you.*

So Naaman goes to visit the king of Israel who was offended and angry at Naaman's request. It was through this reaction that the prophet Elisha knew of Naaman's arrival and request. Only through Naaman experiencing such an overtly negative reaction was he ultimately able to connect with the man God used for healing. We see that he was led to the land because God was able to speak, first through the woman captive in

Aram, and then through the angry reaction in the king of Israel.

Just a side tangent, if I may: Note how Naaman goes with anticipation and a preconceived concept of how he will be healed. In verse ten, Elisha tells Naaman through a messenger to go into the Jordan River, wash himself seven times, and be healed. Verse eleven tells us of Naaman's expectation: to be greeted, to have hands waved over him, and to be proclaimed healed in the name of the Lord.

Do you ever have an expectation of how things are supposed to go and God shows up in your life in an unexpected way?

I know this has happened for me over and over. My first year post injury, I followed medical recommendations to a T. A doctor recommends therapy—I'm there every week. They recommend diet alterations—done. They recommend pharmacological interventions—I follow the prescription. And so on. Over the course of that first year, I got worse, and worse, and worse.

My expectation was to conquer this injury as I had conquered many other challenges in my life. But God showed me that He wanted to work through me and through this injury in a different way. He wanted to heal me and bring me closer to Him. It was only when I released my expectations and began discerning in communion with my God that I began to see and receive how God was using others in my life to bring healing forth in my body, by His design.

In order for Naaman to receive healing, he has to receive the directive and act. This is a reminder to us—God will often provide through our obedience to his directives which are often given through others. Naaman goes on to become angry and refuse to follow the decree. He needs the encouragement of the community traveling with him in order to move forward, which God provides.

And that is when he ultimately decides to act—Naaman goes into the river and dips himself seven times; and he is healed. I can just imagine the discipline it must have taken to dip himself seven times over.

Can you imagine the doubt and frustration that he may have experienced after the third and fourth try with no results?

And then the fifth and sixth try—I imagine anger and rejection must have crept in. But Naaman stayed the course—he followed God's directive with the faith that His instruction would not fail him. And finally, at the seventh dip, he came out of the river with "skin of a young child." (2 Kings 5:14, NLT) God not only healed him of his leprosy—he gave him some anti-aging too! God provides abundantly and his promises never fail.

Led through scripture

Led through a captive

Led through an angry king

Led through a messenger

Led through an expert

Led through a community of encouragement

With the change of his heart and obedience to God's direction, this series of events led to miraculous healing—more than a coincidence! While this story involves human beings as one example, we're living in a time when we have the benefit of having been given this truth directly from Jesus Christ. Jesus tells us before his ascension into heaven that we, the children of God, are now His hands and feet. (John 14:12)

Sometimes, we don't even know how we are being utilized to impact others for the glory of God.

Sometimes, our experience of God moving in our lives isn't necessarily through a person. Sometimes, it's through a song, Mother Nature, a reading, or countless other encounters. Think of one time you noticed this uncanny occurrence in your life.

Can you think of one?

If you are unable to think of one, sit tight. I have complete confidence that God will move in your life in such a way you will experience this pause I'm talking about—challenging you to ask: *Is this more than what it appears?*

I'm reminded of this silly story that's known as The Parable of the Flood. I believe I first heard it from my father. There was a man who was in the path of a grand flood. The floodwaters were coming. He prayed to God while he was in his house to come and save him. *God will come and save me,* he thought. The waters started to rise around his house.

A neighbor came by, urging the man to leave the house, to come with him so he could give him a ride to safety in his truck.

"I'm waiting for God to save me!" answered the man.

His neighbor drove off. The water continued to rise, entering the house. It rose to the point the man had to climb onto the roof for safety. A rowboat came by with people heading to higher ground.

"Come in our boat! We will take you to safety!"

The man said, "No, it's okay. God will save me."

The man continued to pray and the floodwaters continued to rise. A helicopter crew from the Coast Guard flew over. They dropped down a ladder and said over the loudspeaker, "Come on!"

The man waved them on, saying, "No, it's okay. God will save me."

The floodwaters engulfed the man and he drowned. When he arrived in heaven, he asked God, "Why didn't you save me? I believed in you and prayed to you throughout the storm. Why did you let me drown?"

God replied, "I sent you a pickup truck, a boat, and a helicopter, and you refused them all!"

I love how this story depicts God using people in our lives.

God Is Bigger Than Medical Statistics

> *For we are God's handiwork, created in Christ Jesus*
> *to do good works, which God prepared in advance*
> *for us to do.*
> Ephesians 2:10, NIV

The way God heals is holistic, healing the whole being. We currently live with the concept that we can see a specialist for a certain issue, and then we will be treated. Fine. That might be the case. God showed me that we are *connected beings.*

There is scripture to support this:

- Psalm 30
- John 4:14
- John 15:1–5
- Ephesians 2:10

We can't just fix or heal one part of ourselves without our entire selves being changed. This is true even for those who receive miraculous, instant healings through whatever format. Our whole selves are changed by those.

I needed to continue to remind myself that, because I am a whole being, I need to be *all in.* Again, remember that God isn't in the market of bargain shopping for the best deals in you; He's interested in the entire package. He doesn't say some of you is healed in scripture. He says: *You are healed.*

On my healing journey, many statistics were staring me in the face. I'm sure this could be the case for you as well. At the time, statistics were how I operated. I worked in the medical community. Using evidence was how I practiced; it was a method I placed great value on. Then, I reached the point in my healing journey where the statistics no longer indicated healing; they were staring me in the face with evidence that I would live with sickness for the rest of my life. God let me know in my spirit it was not true. *It's not true.*

I was led to understand I am a person—just like you are a person—and not just a number or a statistic. The medical community is often challenged to remember that fact. For a variety of reasons, whatever they may be, humanity can sometimes be limiting.

Humanity is challenged to be able to see past the concrete and to believe in the abstract. Believe in pushing the possibilities into the realm of the impossible. Things that were once thought impossible were only impossible until someone did them. For example, sailing around the world, landing on the moon, running 26.2 miles in under two hours, connecting and communicating with people around the globe instantly, and so on.

I was told by the medical community what my future held according to the data and statistics. I heard lines like: *The percentage of likelihood* or *A recent study suggests someone in your situation is looking at this kind of reality.* I knew something grander.

Doctors told me things like, "You can expect to live with this injury for the rest of your life," and, "It's time to think about acceptance and learning how to cope."

I love how God works through all things; my denial of parts of myself that were still manifesting injury and my need to accept all of me were indeed key to my healing. However, the notion that this was now my life and I needed to figure out how to cope because that's what the statistics suggested was absolutely not what God had in store.

In fact, God took those numbers and told me something that He absolutely intends for you: *I go after every single one of my children. I will leave the ninety-nine to pursue the one. You are not a statistic. Stop keeping your gaze on percentage of likelihood and bring your gaze back to Jesus.*

God was talking to me and leading me to understand that the message of hopelessness I'd received from the doctors was simply not true. It's not true for you either. God has designed each of us in His goodness and has promised complete healing in Jesus's name. (1 Peter 2:24, John 14:13)

You are a precious, unique person whom God loves, and He is ready to give abundantly to you.

God showed me one way He works for healing is with prayer alongside medical interventions. I personally can attest to times in my journey when I underwent a medical intervention with the power of prayers for myself and people praying for me. The results blew the statistics out of the water.

But don't just take my word for it. In her paper, "Meditation, Prayer, and Spiritual Healing: The Evidence," Dr. Marilyn Schlitz writes of the scientific studies and results that document the effects of prayer on medical outcomes, including healing. It's an amazing article that I strongly encourage you to read.

She states:

> It's clear from the correlational studies within the epidemiology data that positive relationships exist between religious and spiritual practice and health outcomes on a variety of different conditions.[1]

In other words, those who are recipients of prayer, positive thoughts, and spiritual practice, do better than those who are not. God has designed us to tap the spiritual alongside our physical. When our whole selves are involved and connected with others' spiritually, we are open to receiving more. God

1 Schlitz, Marilyn. "Meditation, Prayer and Spiritual Healing: The Evidence." *The Permanente Journal* vol. 9, 3 (2005): 63–6. Retrieved from ncbi.nlm.nih.gov/pmc/articles/PMC3396089

is bigger than medical statistics, and prayer is the method by which we can tap His design.

This Is for You Too

And He said to her, "Daughter, your faith has made you well. Go in peace. Your suffering is over."
Mark 5:34

As our Father, God promises us many things, one being complete healing. God's time is God's time and not our time. His design is for God's purpose, which is bigger than anything we can imagine. His design, plans, and purpose are for good (Jeremiah 29:11–13), prosperity, and hope. He is dedicated to you and loves you. He delights in our faith in Him, and our belief and action in that faith brings forth complete healing.

I have shared my story and this truth with many people. More often than not, people don't believe that complete healing is for them. They don't receive it into their hearts. I can relate. God had to work on me before I could realize it was for me. If you don't believe God's gift is for you, I pray you recognize in your heart the response you're having and then go to Him in conversation. He will guide you because He is faithful.

What we are talking about in this book is true. Not only then, but now. Not only for me, but for you. I encourage you to recognize that as humans, we live in the human condition. Being flesh, we have different ways we might receive new information, especially if it challenges our current position, belief, or thought process. And that's okay; it's okay for us to have these lenses. In fact, it's a part of the human design.

The problem occurs when we allow that lens to form our reaction and lead how we then process and live out the information. We have various ways we may receive information, particularly challenging information. Just because we receive it in our human way does not mean it is the be-all and end-all. Having an open mind, an open heart, and honest conversations with God can lead you to understand this gift is for everyone. No exceptions.

And the result?

You will be brought into new depths of life.

CHAPTER TWO

Feel Like You've Tried It All?

YOU'RE NOT DONE YET

This section was birthed from my journey, which didn't go according to plan. In fact, it did not go according to plan at all. I had an injury and, as a result, sustained deficits. I had done my research, completed the diagnostics, and diligently held to a rehabilitation program, all with the objective to overcome the deficits, regain function, and return to life as I'd known it.

As time passed, my drive to make steady progress toward that goal became my daily focus. Everything I did was influenced in some way by my deficits and my attempts to overcome them. But the progress did not play out as I had mapped it, and my function did not return in the time frame I'd designed informed by the research and my medical team.

Yet I was still here. I was still living.

A real battle surfaced within me: *Am I supposed to be here?*

My plan had a different outcome. As I considered the medical reality before me, I began to think I would not receive my outcome.

I was still here—in other words, part of me knew that I had been saved by my Lord Jesus Christ to continue to live on this earth, and at the same time, feeling defeated, another part questioned why?

As I stared at my own arbitrary deadlines for healing, I asked:

- *Did God really have it as part of His design that I was to live the rest of my days strapped in sickness?*

- *Was I supposed to be here for something more? And if so . . . what was that something?*

- *Was I really supposed to have this life at all?*

- *How on Earth could this be what God planned for me?*

- *Why would he spare me to then leave me to live a life feeling broken, incomplete, and a tangled mess?*

I needed to recognize the two sides of this thought process and delve for the answer. I was not able to live a life fulfilled, given where I was in my life. I believed I would be in a place of complete healing by that time. I should have been done. Maybe I was done. The truth of God's biblical promises led me to delve for answers.

Since I believed I was supposed to be here—and I think you are too—I had to search for what to do with the remaining injury and sickness in my life.

At the time, I felt so lonely. I later learned I was not alone. It was a unique and tumultuous thing to be wrestling with— my existence on Earth.

You're not alone in what you may be going through either.

You've Got Breath in Your Body

The indisputable fact is this: You are alive.

Here is a simple breathing exercise, a common meditation practice:

1. Take a moment to make sure you won't be interrupted.

2. Sit comfortably.

3. Close your eyes.

4. Take one deep breath in, feeling how that breath goes in from your nostrils through your nose and the back of your throat into your body.

5. Go ahead and breathe out.

6. Recognize how your body responds to that single breath: the way your chest or stomach moved. Did you become tense anywhere? Did you relax?

7. Take a moment and honor that breath is a core component to life.

Sometimes, we take for granted the basic beauty that is life. Breath is one of the innate and universal, or basic, beauties of life. Start by recognizing these core universal abilities. Breath in your body is a huge and constant reminder that you are alive.

As a believer, we recognize God has designed us in His image and that we are His children. We have the gift of this breath, this moment, this life. God's design is grand and beyond our own understanding, but we have faith in Him and in the purpose He has for each one of us. The Bible tells us of His plans for us before we were even birthed into this world.

> *You made all the delicate, inner parts of my body and knit me together in my mother's womb. Thank you for making me so wonderfully complex! Your workmanship is marvelous—how will I know it.*
> Psalm 139:13–14 NLT

Breath is a constant reminder that air is a resource you can turn to at any time to remind yourself of God's truth. We need those reminders. We need constant access to something real and experiential. That is how we're wired.

You can do the above breathing practice at any time. It is especially helpful to use when you are in a place of battle.

There is real power in our breath, and connecting to it can be an incredibly helpful and centering tool.

In so doing, we connect to a core design of our Creator and Heavenly Father—the reality of our existence in body. This is critically important for the foundation of pursuit of relentless healing.

You Are Shaped, Not Defined, by Your Health

According to Webster's dictionary, *define* means: *To determine or identify the essential qualities or meaning of.* Again, we as believers are first and foremost defined by the love of Christ. Everything else is individualization of that love. This is what I mean by *being shaped.* Your health situation is simply another component to your story shaping how you, as a child of God, are living out the love of Christ. Your health situation is not the essential or core quality of who you are.

One way to live out that truth is by recognizing moments where you think to yourself: *Oh, I can't because of my*—you name it, illness, injury, or deficit. Recognize where in your life you're doing that.

For example, there was a time in my life when I could not read. I would look at a book, and I would experience instant headaches and blurry vision. I was telling others I couldn't read books. Then, I could not read text messages or emails.

I heard myself isolating, having thoughts like: *I would love to reach out to so-and-so, but I can't type out the text* or *I'd love to learn more about such-and-such, but I can't look up the article.* My day was defined by this visual deficit I was experiencing. Defined by it. God led me to a different way of thinking, which is where I changed and started being shaped by it instead.

Instead of saying: *I can't because I* ____, I began to think: *How can I do this while I'm struggling with*____?

See what I did there?

Do you have a deficit impacting your daily life?

Try problem solving around it. Do not let that deficit be your blockade. You can recognize a challenge exists and fervently stand by your ability to access it anyway. You can say: *I am going to find a way to do so.* Then you are not falling victim to your present injury, sickness, or disease.

You can say: *I recognize you, and I am not defined by you.*

Quality of Life

We have established a core with these truths:

- We are defined by being children of God.

- We have access to reminders of His constant provision, such as breathing exercises.

- We are gifted with this moment.

Our next step is recognizing what feels like a blockade and figuring out how to problem solve a way around it based on this core of truths. The result will be an improved quality of life.

I have always been a go-getter. When I reflect on my life, I realize that. Here's an example. At the end of one busy day, I was exhausted. I realized I was on the tail end of several days of feeling that way. Looking over the recent days, I saw that I had filled each moment in pursuit of goals for myself or those I cared about. On the surface, those days were full of accomplishment. But I suddenly saw them with a new lens and realized they were deprived of self-care.

It slapped me in the face that I was spending all my energy, all my resources, and all of me toward things that were taking away from what I truly enjoy about living. I had settled, and I couldn't shake the feeling. I realized I needed to have balance.

I think that is a real challenge in today's society—to recognize what we enjoy about life and not get swept up in exterior pressures or definitions. Instead, we need to focus on what within, and with God, we enjoy about life. We need to examine our balance.

Do you have that healthy balance?

If not, what is preventing it?

I went ahead and wrote it down in two columns.

For you, the columns might be entitled:

1. 1: What activities fill my day?

2. 2: What is it I enjoy about life?

I asked myself these questions and then I reflected on my list and contemplated: *What is impacting my ability to access more of what I enjoy in my life?* I was prayerfully led to navigate a better quality of life. I saw, piece by piece, where I was lacking and how to gain in that area. In other places where I had excess, I understood what I needed to subtract or replace.

And I did it all with the assurance and confidence that none of it was set in stone. I needed to try something, but—like trying out a new pair of pants in the dressing room—if it didn't fit right, I just let it be. This practice was critical as I pursued the medical recommendations God led me to.

When quality of life is increased, there is an increased likelihood to execute medical recommendations. In theory, there are improved outcomes; your ability to reach and receive healing improves.

We have a belief in Jesus and how he healed them all—all people and all sickness, disease, injury, and ailment. You and I are God's adopted children (Galatians 3:26), and therefore have access to His mighty power in our lives. That truth is the core of my faith in Him and my foundation as I pursue the path before me.

It allows me to follow Him and partner with God directly so I can receive God's healing in whatever avenue He has in store. It can be the same for you. We are no different. Remember that because Jesus took it all to the cross (1 Peter 2:24), it is already done. (John 19:30). God showed me that cleaning up the quality of our lives is a critical tool in assisting this process.

I hope this truth is your core as well. Complete healing is already within you. You simply need to access it so it may come forth.

YOUR MIND LEADS; YOUR BODY FOLLOWS

A cheerful heart is good medicine, but a crushed spirit dries up the bones.
Proverbs 17:22, NLT

God led me to the truth that our thoughts are real. When we are thinking them, they exist, but more importantly, they have an impact on who we are and how we receive God's promises, including healing.

Science has caught up with this belief and proved there are vibrational patterns to different thoughts that impact the cellular makeup within our bodies.[2]

Scripture tells us—and science data support—that we are wired for love, positivity, and fruits of the spirit: love, joy, peace, patience, kindness, gentleness, goodness, and self-control.[3] I am continually reminded of the power of my *cheerful heart* and conversely, the power of my *crushed spirit*.

The Woman With the Issue of Bleeding

And a woman was there who had been subject to bleeding for twelve years. She had suffered a great deal under the care of many doctors and had spent all she had, yet instead of getting better she grew worse. When she heard about Jesus, she came up behind him in the crowd and touched his cloak because she thought, "If I just touch his clothes, I will be healed." Immediately her bleeding stopped and she felt in her body that she was freed from her suffering.

---

2 Engel, A.K., P. Fries, and W. Singer. "Dynamic Predictions: Oscillations and Synchrony in Top–Down Processing [Nature Reviews]. Neuroscience, 2001.

3 Lipton, Dr. Bruce. *The Biology of Belief*, Hay House, 2015; Emoto, Dr. Masaru, *The Miracle of Water* (New York, Atria Books, 2011); Galatians 5:22–23.

At once Jesus realized that power had gone out from him. He turned around in the crowd and asked, "Who touched my clothes?"

"You see the people crowding against you," his disciples answered, "and yet you can ask, 'Who touched me?'"

But Jesus kept looking around to see who had done it. Then the woman, knowing what had happened to her, came and fell at his feet and, trembling with fear, told him the whole truth. He said to her, "Daughter, your faith has healed you. Go in peace and be freed from your suffering."

Mark 5:25–34, NIV

Here is a powerful example of the power of the mind. She thought: *If I just touch the hem of his garment, I will be well.*

Did you catch the order there?

She had a thought. She touched his cloak. She received his healing power. Jesus confirmed that her faith had made her well and instructed her to go in peace. In order to have that thought, she first had to have faith. But in order to touch his cloak, she had to have the thought. And her body received what her mind and spirit said.

I was originally introduced to this passage in 2014 through a neuroscientist, Dr. Caroline Leaf, who explained this powerful text in relation to the topic of our mentality and thought process.[4] Jesus is essentially letting us know that we have the power to, with a thought, receive miraculous things. It is so critical we recognize that power.

If we use this woman as an example for our practice of our mind, we understand our mind is the leader and our body follows. She thought the thought and then reached out. I think that we are called to think in kind. We are designed to live in a similar way. We think these thoughts, and then our body follows the path that we are setting for it.

She had suffered for twelve years with constant bleeding, and she could find no cure. Her situation spoke to me because my journey had been longer than I had hoped and was outlasting the predictions of many medical journals. I spent a lot of resources to find healing, and my health, in fact, became worse.

There were personal parallels as well. When I was led to shift my mentality—the way I spoke to myself, my thought process, and how I viewed my life and the world around me—I literally received healing instead. In other words, when I shifted my thought life, my body followed.

Science has begun to provide us with concrete, or *of-this-world*, data to support this reality. In the article, "Neurological Evidence of a Mind-Body Connection: Mindfulness and

---

4 Leaf, Dr. Caroline. "How to Detox Your Brain." YouTube Video. youtube.com/watch?v=WOj66p_JEtE

Pain Control," authors Dr. Raymond St. Marie and Kellie S. Talebkhah review the changes in our brain (body part) in people who use meditative techniques (mind) for pain control.[5] The article provides a wonderful overview of studies that have proven the brain acts differently when the person is thinking differently—to the point of alleviating painful stimuli.

This is simply one example supporting the powerful reality of how God has designed us.

Quantum Physics

I love when God opens a window into His design through scientific data. To further my understanding, God led me to the study of quantum physics. It became another resource outside the Bible. We are all connected, and we all vibrate and are influenced by vibrations.

To bring us back to high school physics, I'd like to share an example. Everything—from a thought to building—has a vibrational pattern. There is another study about thoughts and how they impact the molecular structure of water. Dr. Masaru Emoto provided this information about the way

---

5 St. Marie, Raymond, and Kellie S. Talebkhah. "Neurological Evidence of a Mind-Body Connection: Mindfulness and Pain Control." *The American Journal of Psychiatry Residents' Journal*. April 2018. Retrieved from psychiatryonline.org/doi/pdf/10.1176/appi.ajp-rj.2018.130401

water molecules crystalize in response to positive language.[6] You can find pictures of these changes online. Beautiful crystals!

I love you was one thought he focused on, versus *I hate you*. When frozen, the *I love you* water displayed beautiful crystals, works of art. The *I hate you* water displayed broken, ugly-looking, harder-to-look-at crystals. The science tells us we are impacted by vibrational patterns, and physics tells us everything vibrates at some level.

Additionally, we have Dr. Emoto's research showing positive versus negative thoughts significantly impacted the molecular structure of water molecules. We human beings are mostly water. If we have positive thoughts, we are significantly impacting and promoting positive and optimal expression of our bodies.

Who surrounds you?

Who is on your team in your healing journey?

The answers to these questions matter. The people around you impact how you live and how you receive the gift of life, for their words, intentions, and so on have vibrational patterns. Patterns that will impact not only your thoughts, but your state of being and, in turn, your cellular makeup. We are all connected.

---

6 Emoto, Masaru. *The Hidden Messages in Water*. New York: Atria Books, 2001.

Scripture tells us that we believe from hearing; not from having heard. I believe that part of this charge is a call to actively seek out a way to receive vibrational patterns of love and the goodness of God. Not only in the people who surround us, but in the pasttimes we keep, the environment we live in, and the food and drink we consume. All of these factors influence our own vibrations, and in turn, our own mind and internal monologue which, by God's design, we have a responsibility to receive.

> *I want them to be encouraged and knit together by the strong ties of love.*
> Colossians 2:2, NLT

> *Now you are the body of Christ and individually members of it.*
> 1 Corinthians 12:27, ESV

It Really Is Real

Cassandra Vieten, PhD, in her TEDx presentation, "The Science of Interconnectedness," discusses the very real and undeniable data that we are all connected not only to all of humankind, but to all the world.[7] Who we are is not only impacted by our state of being, but by others' as well.

---

7 Vieten, Cassandra. "The Science of Interconnectedness." *TEDx*. YouTube Video, Feb 2, 2016. https://www.youtube.com/watch?v=eEd_YTZB1Tw

Cassandra talks about how our DNA is no longer viewed as a blueprint for who we are and who we will become, but is rather significantly impacted by our interactions with others and our state of mind. So, I believe if we keep in the word, take part in practices that claim God's complete healing, maintain an environment that makes us successful in bringing forth such healing, we can be good stewards of God's calling. I believe this positions us for the greatest success—as many scientific studies, in quantum physics and traditional science, have begun to reveal.

It is tempting to hear this information and think: *It's thought-provoking; it's worth thinking about.*

I agree. All too often, however, when I have been led to share this with others, I find this is where thinking stops. Sometimes it's not even received well.

Either way, it's meant to be received and lived out. I encourage you not to take my word for it. Look up the sources online, reach out to others, and find out for yourself. If you pursue greater understanding, I know you will find what I'm saying is real and true. There are many testimonies to back it up.

I was just reminded of an exercise about an expression of the positive influence of your mind on your body.

Please take a second to read this exercise, and then do it as it is an awesome and quick experiment to explore the miraculous power of our minds:

- First, stand up and grab a partner.

- Next, stay standing and extend both arms out straight on either side of you so they are parallel to the floor. Your right arm should be extended straight out to your right, left arm to the left. Palms face up. Eyes closed.

- Now, think of something that is really stressing you out. First thing that comes to mind.

- Nod your head to signal to your partner that you are holding the thought.

- Continue thinking about the stressful thought, and as you do, your partner can come over and push on your arms with reasonable force so they fall down.

- Next, repeat the stance: arms out, palms up, eyes closed. Then think of something positive, something that brings you joy, something that helps you come alive. Once you have it, nod your head to your partner.

- Your partner should push down on your arms with the same amount of force as the first time.

- Go ahead and take a step back.

I think you may find that they were unable to press your arms down.

What?

This exercise is a pretty cool way to experience the power of your thoughts on your body.

Remember Proverbs 17:22? *A cheerful heart is good medicine, but a crushed spirit dries up the bones.* (NLT) God has designed us in such a way that we are wired for positivity. With such vibrations running through our bodies, we have greater expression of who we are designed to be, including things like body function and inner strength.

WILLING TO BE SCULPTED

The saying has been around for a long time: *He is the potter; I am the clay.*

Every time I hear it, I see an image of a potter with a hunk of clay on the wheel and their hands covered in clay. It's a mess around the wheel and around their hands—clay under their fingernails and between their fingers. However, the lump at the center that started as a hunk of clay takes shape. I continue to watch it become something unique and beautiful.

When we commit our whole self to our savior and live out our days in pursuit of His promises, I believe we begin the journey of being sculpted. We need humility and the grounded understanding that He is the creator of all. He is trustworthy and so is His design in shaping who we are.

We have come to this place in our understanding:

- We recognize our body is God's beautiful design and His tabernacle.

- We believe in being connected to all things.

- We witness the power of the mind and the impact of positive mental states and vibrational patterns.

Now, let's delve into the components of how change happens.

He Is the Potter; I Am the Clay

In our earthly life, it is tempting to feel like it is *our* health and well-being; and therefore, the responsibility for health rests on our own shoulders. Instead, we need to recognize it's about the partnership between our savior and ourselves. And with that partnership comes the release of ownership and trust in our Creator's hands. Allowing God to take the lead results in the fulfillment in us of His ultimate design.

Remember, God tells us that our body is His vessel, His temple. We are designed to be in continuous partnership with Him, deeply and spiritually. Dr. Caroline Leaf tells us that science now shows that our minds are to be focused on God every ten seconds of every waking moment.[8] We are called to be active participants, but it is not our decision alone dictating our fate. Our creator is intimately and actively involved.

8 Leaf, Dr. Caroline. "Mind-Body Connection". YouTube Video, February 27, 2017. https://www.youtube.com/watch?v=skh2iAr8SWc

In recognizing that relationship, it is important to develop discernment and prayer practices to live out and execute that which is before you. With these practices, we can be shaped and developed into the full beauty God has in store for us. This is such good news! God's design is greater than anything we could ever build on our own. We will delve into discernment later in this book, but a tool to explore might be something like Dr. Caroline Leaf's app, theswitch.app.

The Resistance Within

This call to release all of me into the hands of God with no inhibitions—no holding back—was extremely challenging for me. At a time when I felt like I had developed strategies and systems to hold it together, God was telling me to let it all go and let Him take over. Looking back, I now see that my systems and strategies were making me functional, but I was not experiencing the fullness of what life had to offer.

But I had worked hard at developing these systems. I was keenly aware of my needs and how various variables in my environment would impact me. Such things gave me this sense of control. So, when God revealed to me the truths we just discussed, I was terrified. These strategies were my safety nets when things suddenly took a turn; my shields from challenging occurrences; my comfort when I felt broken. Not only was I terrified, but I didn't know how to function without them.

But I was no longer *moldable* by our God the potter. I needed to let go of all of those systems and strategies because they had become so intertwined with my identity. In other words, I had slipped into focus on my strategies and not on Him. Scripture refers to such a mentality as *idols.* God is very clear in scripture that there is no other God but Him, and that we are to relinquish all idols in order to live life in the fullness of God.

Needless to say, I was extremely resistant to allowing God to mold all of me. And I wonder if maybe you are feeling some resistance yourself?

What are your personal cues that you are experiencing resistance?

I am sharing a 100 percent honest moment. Even talking about this subject, I can feel agitation rising up in me. That agitation then builds into mentally huffing and puffing and feeling like I don't want to do a thing.

Then, my thoughts start to morph into:

- Acceptance of sickness: *I'm fine living with headaches.*

- Comparison to others: *I'm a lot better off than her.*

- Feelings of never-ending work: *Am I chasing an unattainable goal?*

That first sign of agitation is a red flag that I need to take a moment. I need to remember we are all human, and part of being human is recognizing we are incomplete without our partnership with God. In order for this partnership to work, we must fully accept and proclaim His promises in us and our life. It is important to start a practice of recognizing your cues that you are experiencing resistance. That is step number one.

If step number one is to recognize resistance, step number two is to accept its presence. I am always delighted when science backs up what God has claimed for centuries. There is scientific evidence now that we are neurologically wired to go the path of least resistance, especially in our bodies.[9]

What I am talking about here is *flying in the face of easy*. We should recognize resistance is going to be a part of this journey. We can be okay with that. Often I find that in recognizing it, we take its power away. So many times, we hit that resistance within, and we say *It's not for me, that's not how I'm wired. I tried and it was too hard.* We need to hold it and say: *This is a part of my journey too.* It doesn't mean that is the end of this journey.

Instead, try saying something like: *This resistance is because I am starting something new or pursuing something greater.* Whatever affirmation you need, claim it, write it down, pray about it, and talk about it. Bringing awareness and discussion

9 Hagura, Nobuhiro; Patrick Haggard, and Jörn Diedrichsen. "Perceptual Decisions Are Biased by the Cost to Act." *eLife*, February 2017. doi: 10.7554/eLife.18422.001

to resistance is exactly what we need to do to disarm its power so we can move forward.

The third step is to discuss it with God. The result will often be the ability to loosen the grip of resistance on your mind. Often, this practice needs to happen repeatedly. Then, we experience a wonderful byproduct of the goal: recognition of resistance so we may receive God's hand sculpting us into His design.

We also experience external resistance.

Some examples might be things we've already chatted about:

- Medical professionals advising you to accept sickness
- Someone expressing their doubt into your situation
- Physical distance from a uniquely equipped person

External resistance should be recognized and is not necessarily the be-all and end-all.

Use the same practice I outlined for internal resistance:

1. Recognition
2. Acceptance and understanding
3. Discussion

Sometimes external resistance guides you in a different direction or a detoured direction. Very rarely is resistance, internal or external, something from God saying: *No, that promise you are pursuing is not what I have in store for you.* This process, however, can become a catalyst to a deeper expression of your faith and is critical to the ability to welcome God's sculpting hand.

Change Is a Reality of Life

> *Human beings are works in progress that*
> *mistakenly think they're finished . . . The one*
> *constant in our lives is change.*
> ~ Daniel Gilbert, author
> *Stumbling on Happiness*

Many of us hit a certain point in adulthood at which we feel we are not changing all that much. Sometimes we feel like we've reached the proverbial *goal line*, and we are finished changing. I think it's easier to look at children, for example, and see change; they have grown another inch, or we have to trim their nails. Change happens so rapidly in children, especially young ones and teenagers.

In comparison, we feel as adults that we don't change anymore. The fact is we absolutely do. Our changes might be a little more covert. First of all, physically there are still changes. Our nails still need to get clipped; our hair still grows.

There is also consistent, constant change in our surroundings. I love nature. To see the seasons change from spring to summer to fall to winter is a nice reminder—particularly in those transitional months between seasons—that our world is always changing. There is a cycle to nature and this world.

"Seasons" is a wise metaphor for the movement
of life, I think. It suggests that life is neither a
battlefield nor a game of chance but something
infinitely richer, more promising, more real. The
notion that our lives are like the eternal cycle of
the seasons does not deny the struggle or the joy,
the loss or the gain, the darkness or the light, but
encourages us to embrace it all—and to find in all of
it opportunities for growth.[10]

~ Parker Palmer

With recognition that life is a constant change—and all that can come as a result—it is safe for us to bridge this reality to the change that manifests in our bodies.

In his book, *The Slight Edge*, Jeff Olson talks about change, the makeup of it, and the fact that it happens whether or not you choose to recognize it. (Momentum Media, 2005) Either way is fine, but it is there. He encourages us to recognize it because it is in that recognition that we know how to use such change to our advantage. Jeff states that falling victim to change is the other option.

What I am asking you to do is honor that change
exists. When you do honor it and make life choices

---

10 Palmer, Parker. "Seasons: A Center for Renewal." *Fetzer Institute.* Retrieved from fetzer.org/sites/default/files/images/stories/pdf/seasonsbook.pdf

*with that in mind, you are not going to be a victim
to the change.*

When you do not honor that change exists, you can suddenly find you are fifty years down the line, and you don't know where the time went and what you are going to do. You didn't plan for this situation. Most of the time, you won't see changes that are percolating, if you resist embracing this truth.

When you can live and embrace the change, you can empower yourself to pursue the path that God is leading you toward because you will have faith and trust that His plan and His design are for healing and goodness in your life.

Here are some practices that might be helpful for you to execute some of what we talked about in this chapter:

1. Set aside five minutes of prayer time to allow for discernment when recognizing that God is the potter and you are the clay.

2. Put a small notebook in your purse or pocket with a small pen or use a notetaking app on your smartphone to quickly jot down feelings of resistance and where you felt them in your body.

3. Bring these notes to your prayer time with God.

Change is our reality and needs to be recognized as much as resistance. Recognize and accept what is before you. Then ask yourself what you want in that area. Confirm to yourself you are proclaiming a spiritual truth. Prayerfully ask God what steps are needed in order to bring about that change in your life. Now you're being molded!

CHAPTER THREE

Navigating the Healthcare System

THE ROLE OF HEALTH INSURANCE

The phrase *health insurance* is like a curse word. I feel like I can barely say it without rolling my eyes. People hear it these days, and I immediately sense stress. My hope in this section is to recognize that stress and honor it but also work through why we feel it and how to live with health insurance.

What It Is Today

It is challenging to define health insurance in a way that will not inevitably become outdated. In the political season we are in, our healthcare system operates as fluid—meaning change is inevitable. We are always needing to adapt. Maybe that is the way it will be from here forward.

At one point in our American history, health insurance was not this fluid, ever-dynamic component of life. There was a time in our culture when health insurance was extremely constant and reliable. Everyone would have defined it similarly: we were able to receive the healthcare we needed with no thought as to whether it would be available to us and paid for.

Additionally, we did not necessarily have to pay out of pocket to receive it. We had already done our part in our deductions out of our pay check. In other words, insurance coverage was at 100 percent, and deductibles were a blink of the eye.

Let's empower ourselves and briefly review some core terminology in regard to health insurance.

Coverage: This references the services your health insurance company is willing to help pay for based on your plan agreement. The company will often outline different procedures and types of medical professionals that will be covered and will outline how many visits or how much time and money is allowed by the plan. They will also outline how much they are willing to cover and how much you are expected to pay.

For example, you might have an 80/20 plan. This means insurance will pay for 80 percent of the charges and you are expected to pay for 20 percent of the charges billed for the service rendered after your deductible has been met. A copy of your coverage is often available via your insurance provider's website, or you may request a printed copy.

Reimbursement: Insurance pays for the services rendered after they have been provided. Therefore, the paying party or servicing party is reimbursed by the insurance company for such services as coverage allows under your individual plan.

In-Network: Medical professionals who have agreed to accept your insurance provider's rates of reimbursement. A common tag line here is that they *accept ____ insurance* or are *participants with ____ insurance*. Your coverage is different when you choose medical providers in-network versus out-of-network. It is important to know the difference in coverage as well as whether a medical provider is in- versus out-of-network.

Out-of-Network: Medical professionals who have not contracted with your insurance provider to agree to their terms. This is a different level of insurance coverage; however, different does not mean *not an option*.

Simple questions to ask medical providers include:

Do you accept my insurance?

If not: *What is your policy for servicing patients who are considered out-of-network?*

For example, you might ask: *Do you provide documentation so I may submit it to my insurance for reimbursement?*

Have documentation and know your insurance provider's agreement for out-of-network coverage and how this may impact your personal expenses. For example, your plan might be 50/50.

Deductions: The cost of your insurance plan. If your coverage is through your employer, it is the amount of money taken directly from your paycheck.

Deductible: The amount of money paid by you before your insurance coverage kicks in.

Out-of-Pocket Max: The capped amount of money you must pay for medical care as authorized by your insurance provider.

CPT codes: The codes used by the healthcare industry to classify medical procedures. For example, one type of a speech therapy session could be coded as CPT code 92507. These are good for you to know when you want to research if a certain procedure is covered under your plan.

ICD-10 codes: Diagnostic coding for the specific ailments being targeted. Someone who has swallowing difficulties, for example, might have a condition defined as dysphagia, which could be coded ICD-10 R13.10.

Understanding this terminology is critical in empowering ourselves to be good stewards in executing the plan God puts before us. We will explore how to use information like this a little later.

Culturally, we have continued to believe the constant of wonderful healthcare coverage at low low rates was going to be there. The reality is that the economics of it were not sustainable, and coverage began to change.

Most people find the topic so dry, they fall asleep. Needless to say, coverage had to change. We are in a season when we are living out that tipping point. Now, we need to recognize that deductions are simply the beginning. That is just our entry ticket. In order to receive, there are additional monies that will go into care for a majority of health insurance coverage out there.

It Is a Resource, Not a Barrier, to Healing

Healthcare is a business; people want to make money. We need to understand there are many rules and regulations health insurance companies have in place that we must meet for claims adjusters to deem it appropriate to cover whatever medical service we have received.

We need to realize something important and revolutionary: *Health insurance companies are not the ones to decide what we receive for our healing.* Remember you are already healed in Jesus's name, and it is God who is leading you in the expression of that healing. So, when God leads us toward an avenue that our health insurance company may not embrace, we are called to see that avenue with new eyes.

Honor that healing is something God is longing for in your life and explore additional ways to be able to pursue that path. In my journey, for example, I was led to the first specialist my insurance company considered out-of-network. Truly, the way I heard *they don't accept my insurance*—meaning out-of-network provider—was *I cannot be seen by this provider. I am not accepted at this clinic.*

In your heart, you can know an avenue is something God is leading you to receive for your healing. In my case, I went ahead and pursued it. I figured out how to make it happen by the grace of God, and I received the service. On the other end, I was told by the health insurance company they did not find it appropriate for me to receive that service, so they were not going to cover it.

I knew I was going to have to pay for the whole thing out of pocket. It's vital that you recognize that health insurance companies are meant to be utilized, but they do not get to say what type of medical intervention you receive. God gets to say that, and you can follow.

When you receive this type of information or denials from insurances, do not simply bow down and say: *Well, that path is not something I am meant to pursue because of what my health insurance coverage is.* That is not God's design, and that is not how you are meant to live it out. There are many other options. And as God intends it for your life, He will provide.

Communicating With Health Insurance Companies

Two things come to mind: The first thing we need to understand when talking with a health insurance representative is this: while you are talking to a human being, there is a strict structure and format involved in framing the way you are communicating with them. I worked hard to understand and figure out how to navigate this structure because it was deeply irritating and frustrating.

But, I needed to talk to these people. I needed to figure out a way. That was where it started. That was where it was meant to start: recognition and understanding.

You might be talking with somebody who is a beautiful, wonderful person, created in God's image, but there is an invisible structure they are navigating with you. Once I understood that, I needed to figure out the basics. I felt encouraged, like we were on similar wavelengths. Understand that they are always going to need to confirm your identity even though you already gave it all in the automated portion of the call. Preface delving into your questions with a quick plug of how many things you need to talk about; i.e., *I have two questions today.* Be prepared with specifics such as dates and names of providers. When they use terms you don't know, ask them for a definition.

They used vocabulary I had to learn. I had to look up definitions for words and examples. I wrote down the terminology I learned and practiced using it in sentences.

Doing so prepared me to effectively communicate my needs with the insurance representatives. Otherwise, we were not speaking the same language.

In the mode of verbal communication, this learning is essential. Always ask whom you are speaking to and write down their name. Ask if they have a direct line or extension you can use in the future to follow up with them directly. Ask if there's a case number for the call and date it so you can streamline reference to it in future callbacks if needed.

Next, document on your own. They are recording and documenting. They tell you that every time over the phone. Empower yourself because you talk to a different person almost every time. You need a running record to be successful in delving into this information gathering or communicating with them.

Sometimes, answers are provided in one call, and it's wonderful when that happens. When you start investigating or following up on a denial, that is when solutions take more than one phone call—multiple phone calls and paperwork. It's important that you document and organize yourself because it can become confusing.

Often, people throw up their hands and say: *Forget it*.

We are using health insurance as a resource, and we need to go ahead and use it. We can't just say: *This is aggravating*.

Forget it. If we give up, we are not necessarily following the task put before us. That is not acceptable.

My hope is to shake off the thought that health insurance is an unnecessary evil in our world. Instead, I want you to understand these persons are a resource you need to understand and utilize.

> *Do your best to present yourself to God as one*
> *approved, a worker who has no need to be ashamed,*
> *rightly handling the word of truth.*
>   2 Timothy 2:15, ESV

GOD USES MANY HANDS

We are God's hands and feet now. This is the reality since Jesus ascended into heaven. Its application crosses many contexts in life. It is definitely applicable when it comes to your healing.

> *We are therefore Christ's ambassadors as though*
> *God were making his appeal through us.*
>   2 Corinthians 5:20, NIV

Medical Professionals

This is a tough topic for me: medical professionals versus nonmedical professionals. I know it is a touchy subject in the Christian community and in the non-Christian community as well. There are lots of schools of thought and different sides of the argument about whether God has written we are in need of certain types of care and not in need of other types of care. I recognize that. I honor it.

There are some who are of the opinion that because Jesus healed so miraculously and instantly, there is no place for medical professionals in our healing. There are others who feel that those who offer healing through nontraditional means are going against Christian beliefs and are somehow forbidden.

It's critical we look at the core of why we come to certain opinions. To me, when I hear the opinion about the reasons you need to go to a medical professional, I often hear a lot of misunderstanding. As we continue, I encourage you to have an open heart and an open mind. Allow God to show you what lies at the core of your feelings toward these two schools of thought.

I was told certain types of medical professional intervention I received from the community were a complete waste—there was no need for them. Other people are entitled to their opinion; however, I recognize in my heart these interventions were exactly what I needed.

As you move forward, grab assurance from God and hold onto it. He'll give it to you. It's on you to set yourself up for success and move forward. Let the external hypocrites fall on deaf ears, or at least bring them to God so you can discern and receive clarity in your soul.

It took me a while to recognize God is in many clinical settings. I often thought of them as places where I needed to gear up for battle. I thought I needed to be ready to fight an *of-this-world* fight. I would do a lot of research and preparation and arrive with my whole bag, armed and ready.

While it was important to be prepared for these appointments, I ended up learning that my true tasks were more about discernment and recognition. I needed to be able to recognize whether I was meant to work with an institution or move on. The work of trusting in that discernment, recognizing when a season has ended, and understanding each event as a drop in the bucket, moved me forward in some way.

While sometimes you might not do what the clinician is recommending, that's okay. Just because someone has on a white coat and is telling you something doesn't necessarily make that the be-all and end-all for you. I think so many medical professionals are very well-educated and smart, but they are human just like you.

In my own experience, I realized gearing up for every appointment was sourced in pain and trauma from previously misguided healthcare interventions. I was led to the process of forgiveness. I had to address every past interaction I felt was a wrongdoing and forgive them. It was only through this forgiveness I was set free from the anxiety of stepping foot in a medical professional's arena. Through this process, I was able to connect with my soul and grow in my discernment.

I encourage you to connect with God and heal some experiences that were not helpful or perhaps traumatic. I can relate to those experiences deeply.

Remember that God is the grand physician, and in being such, experts of all kinds here on Earth pale in comparison to the individualized knowledge of our God. Take a moment to bring to Him any experiences that are surrounded by hurt. For to be told medical opinions that are simply misguided is a unique type of pain. And if you were at all like me and followed the misguided advice and referrals to more professionals who were operating under misguided information, well, now you're really in a web of pain and confusion!

What I encourage instead is gratitude and empowerment. Be grateful you have a better source, *the* Source of all things, leading and speaking to you. He empowers you to receive His design and His power.

When God does use medical professionals for your healing, he will confirm it for you in a way only God can. And when He does, the feeling of reassurance is miraculous. Remember God is God, and He will do what He wants to do in you through others, no matter of their intentions. He is the great I AM.

Nonmedical Professionals

After my injury, my life was about the use of medical professionals. Having trained and worked as a medical professional for my entire adult life, that was the only way I viewed healing. I had ailments that needed physical therapy, so I needed to go see a physical therapist. I had an injury to my brain, so I needed to see a neurologist. I had vision difficulties, so I needed to see an eye doctor. These were my symptoms, so these were the specialists I needed to see for them. In my focal viewpoint, that is how I was going to get better.

God opened my eyes to see I am a whole person. He is about our whole selves. In longing to heal all of you, all of me, He designs something that involves and touches the lives of many people. There is a critical need for support and community, if for nothing else than connection and receiving love.

Remember our quantum physics?

We are designed to have and live with positive thoughts, love, and healing. (Philippians 4:8) God started to shed light for me on this spiritual world, the different types and the power of prayer, the laying on of hands, and the different types of healing.

I came to understand many different ways He envelopes us and communicates with us:

- Support groups
- Music
- Poetry
- Painting
- Workout groups
- Continuing education classes

The list is endless, as is God's design. Again, I encourage you to search your heart, recognize how this is resonating with you, and take some time with God to listen.

What needs to be worked through between the two of you?

What did I do?

I had a mentor. I read books. I found podcasts. Watched YouTube videos.

I accessed many resources:

- Worship songs and bands
- Online prayer resources
- Support groups in my physical community

I picked up the phone and called people who weren't physically present with me. I explored artistic avenues I read about and then shared them with my close, confidant tribe.

I felt the hand of God leading me toward sources. I gathered information from them. Then, I turned to various places for support and counsel, depending on where I was in my journey. I also had quiet practices that helped me process it all.

See, the Lord uses it all. All for His glory in you—His temple.

It was with the addition of these resources, people, and practices that my healing took on an even grander form. I began to feel my whole self, awakening and growing into the best expression of me.

Book of Acts: The Disciples Healed After Jesus' Ascension

This might make me a bad Christian, but I hadn't ever given a lot of thought to the Book of Acts. I hadn't read it. I thought of it as the story of setting up churches and divisions among groups. I am grateful. God is good. He led me to understand there is so much more in the book.

There are amazing stories about miraculous powers of God accomplished through the disciples. Not just one of the disciples, but many, who performed miracles. These are the stories of many instances in which people receive healing.

For some examples, read:

- Acts 3:1–10
- Acts 5:12–16
- Acts 8: 4–8
- Acts 9:33–34
- Acts 9: 3–42

- Acts 14:8–10
- Acts 16:16–18
- Acts 19:11–12
- Acts 20:9–12
- Acts 28:7–9

> *And his name—by faith in his name—has made this man strong whom you see and know, and the faith that is through Jesus has given the man this perfect health in the presence of you all.*
> Acts 3:16, ESV

That powerful realization helped me receive God's healing and live out the healing as it came forth. It created a new reality for me. This was not simply a charge Jesus gave each of us—although, yes, it was that. It was a directive that was fulfilled through his followers. Time and time again.

I began to understand this kind of work is alive today. I had no idea. It opened an entire world for me as I realized how Jesus moves in our lives and in our world. As we are continuing to pursue our healing path, we need these reminders and resources right at our fingertips because the journey is not easy.

What better place to go to than God's words?

What I love about the current age is you can find these words easily by researching online and going to the back of a Bible. You can also find reputable commentaries that expand on it. You can find talks that apply it to today. One biblical story might be a platform for understanding in a variety of different ways.

The Book of Acts has been a critical component for me in my pursuit of knowing how God is moving in my life and whose hands He is guiding me toward. It is evidence of His hands at work through His children. I encourage you to open up this book throughout your journey, but particularly if you find yourself in a mindset of doubt. My hope is that scripture will speak to your doubt and become the catalyst for prayer, discernment, and action in your life.

THE REALITY OF PAYMENT

When we can release and put things into God's hands, He absolutely responds in kind. When it comes to money, we are called to be good stewards of it. I think a book about healing that does not discuss the inevitability of items and services that will need to be paid for would be remiss. So, here's my humble attempt.

How Healthcare Bills Are Different

The healthcare bills just kept on coming. My memory paints a picture at this time in my life of our pedestal table swarmed with ever-growing piles of paperwork—bills and bills and bills—like in the cartoons when you see stacks of paper with no end in sight. It was an overwhelming feeling. How was I going to do this on top of everything else?

Through this book, you will be more equipped because you are going to have a better understanding of your insurance coverage and what kind of financial situations you might be up against prior to them arriving at your doorstep.

I was able to understand that healthcare bills, while they may look similar to an electric bill or a water bill, are, in fact, a bit different. Depending on your situation, there are various options. I strongly encourage you to call the medical institution and talk to a representative if you receive a bill way out of your ability to manage financially. They have personnel on staff ready to talk to people who have difficulty paying healthcare bills. I had no idea. They can help. They can help you address it.

I learned another lesson completely by accident. I received a bill for a lot of money. I didn't have enough money to pay all of it, but I did have enough money to pay some of it. I figured I was going to pay what I could pay. That's what I did. The following month, a bill came with a new due date, and the amount owed had my previous payment subtracted from it. I thought I hacked the system! Turns out—you can do that!

Officially, it's best to set it up with the medical institution so everyone is on the same page. There are scary due dates on these bills. An electricity company can turn off your electricity if the bill still isn't paid past the due date. When it comes to your healthcare, it is simply unethical for them to impose some sort of ramification. There is more to these bills than meets the eye. You need to be an active participant to fully wrap your head around everything involved.

There are three key steps to respond to a large medical bill:

1. Call the medical institution to confirm the charges on the bill and clarify the services rendered as documented on the bill. Ask what CPT codes are being billed and what ICD-10 diagnoses are documented in preparation for step 2.

2. Call your insurance company to confirm the portion that you are being billed for is appropriate.

3. Set up a plan that allows you to financially stomach the bill.

The Importance of a Budget

> *But don't begin until you count the cost. For who would begin construction of a building without first calculating the cost to see if there is enough money to finish it? Otherwise, you might complete only the foundation before running out of money, and then everyone would laugh at you. They would say, "There's the person who started that building and couldn't afford to finish it!"*

Luke 14:28–30, NLT

My husband and I were led to Dave Ramsey's Financial Peace University class one year prior to my injury. Only by God's design would we have been prepared to "live like no one else, so that later we can live and give like no one else," as Dave Ramsey says.

I highly recommend his course. In our life, it has been the foundation for being good stewards of our money—yes. But more than that, it gave us a system to work together as a team when it comes to finances. It helped us use money as a tool and not let money dictate our decision making.

The use of a budget is empowering. A budget provides a framework to tell your money where to go. Understand your finances. Live in a way that makes you feel confident in your financial situation.

Medical bills are the number one source of bankruptcy in America. But debt is not God's design. (Proverbs 22:7) Instead, he empowers us to be good stewards of our money with our spirits of power, love, and sound mind. (2 Timothy 1:7)

When you are figuring out how to pay these healthcare bills, you need to know what you're working with. Being a steward of money is critical. The more people I talked to, the more I realized they felt like their financial situation was constraining them to pursue the path before them. They found the bills so oppressive they were frozen and helpless, not knowing how to attack them.

That feeling, quite simply, is not God's design. That is why a budget is so important. It is a tool to empower ourselves to be good stewards of the gifts God has given us and to follow His lead in our lives. For more information, I recommend exploring Dave Ramsey's website: www.daveramsey.com/get-started/financial-action-plan

Investing in Yourself

> *The LORD will send rain at the proper time from his rich treasury in the heavens and will bless all the work you do. You will lend to many nations, but you will never need to borrow from them.*
> Deuteronomy 28:12, NLT

> *Wisdom and money can get you almost anything, but only wisdom can save your life.*
> Ecclesiastes 7:12 NLT

When considering the numbers in our budget as we look at these healthcare bills pouring in, we can be tempted to think: *I am spending a lot of money here. Is it really worth it?* This question is based in doubt and uncertainty—two big red flags signaling we have something in our hearts we need to go to God about. Those two emotions are not of the Spirit.

Remember the fruits of the Spirit?

But the fruit of the Spirit is love, joy, peace, patience, kindness, goodness, faithfulness, gentleness, and self-control. (Galatians 5:22–23 (NLT)

Understand we are of God's design, we are one body, and we are His holy temple. So, when you start to question your investment in yourself, it is important to recognize and honor that concern. Let the Holy Spirit counsel you.

For the reality is this: *We are given one body, one life, and that's it.*

And, you are uniquely designed. You have a precious purpose and you are worth it. What you have to offer is invaluable. It's to be celebrated, invested in, and lived out in all its grandeur.

Our culture provides images of what we want to spend money on. In no way is it ever on healthcare bills. That simply is not talked about. But to live out the gift of the day that God has given, you need to be your best you. That doesn't always come for free. That's okay. God gifts us with the resources we need, along with the knowledge and ability to access such resources. It is on us to pursue them.

I need to bring this issue to God continuously. It is a regular part of what He and I talk about. He brings me to the truth that I am His child. He loves me. He wants what's best for me, and what's best for you.

Don't let finances stand in the way of participating in the path before you. If God means something for you, He provides a way. We must simply be openhearted to the way He moves.

CHAPTER FOUR

How to Discern God's Lead— A Practical Application

GUT FEELINGS

I realized this chapter is a handbook of what I found effective in bridging the spiritual side of my understanding of healing—God's promise of complete healing in Jesus's name—and the use of it in this world. I discovered that a simple gut feeling is a core spark ignited time and time again in this process.

Defining Gut Feelings

> *Gut feeling* (noun) (plural: gut feelings) (idiomatic): an instinct or intuition; an immediate or basic feeling or reaction without a logical rationale (Webster's Dictionary).

As a whole, our American culture does not give a lot of weight to gut feelings. Our medical field is all about evidence-based practice (EBP). The highest standard of care is providing care to a patient using a delineated process and procedure and research-backed data to support the course of action. I agree that this is an excellent model of care and support it in many facets of our healthcare industry.

I still base my clinical decisions in this method when working as a speech-language pathologist. Asking about evidence behind courses of action for my own personal care is a critical piece in my decision making. However, I found for me, EBP was what I turned to in place of listening to my inner self-speak.

Instead of honoring both sides, I denied my inner voice and didn't really understand the way my gut feelings were leading me. Instead, I turned to a linear plan as outlined in the many medical recommendations I received. As a result, I truly fell victim to the symptoms and sensations I felt. While my inner voice was crying out, my mind was seeking understanding from the external. Because of my life history and my injury, I had little understanding of gut feelings. So, they really never stood a chance in those early days.

I had to redefine *gut feeling*. I had to experience the power of how right and reliable a gut feeling is. I took a leap of faith. If you are in a similar place, it will take your own leap of faith to give it a try.

Believe it or not, there is a lot of research about gut feelings and other people's journeys. I pored over that research.[11] It was simple, and it's something you can absolutely do on your own time. For me, I landed at the end of the Webster's dictionary definition: a reaction without a logical rationale.

Through experience, I began to trust in other actions of my mind and brain's capacity—beyond the logical. I learned that even though gut feelings didn't fit in a format the logical side of my brain comprehended, it didn't mean they weren't real, worthwhile, or powerfully present.

Gut feelings manifest in my body in different ways. Many of those ways are universal, and I hope can provide a starting place for you.

Some of the signs may include visceral knowing, such as:

- An increased pulse rate or heart palpitations
- Tensing around the neck or jawline
- Sitting up a little straighter

---

11 Lufityanto, G., C. Donkin, and J. Pearson. "Measuring Intuition: Nonconscious Emotional Information Boosts Decision Accuracy and Confidence." *Psychological Science* (2016). doi: 10.1177/0956797616629403; Stevenson, S. and R. Hicks. "Trust Your Instincts: The Relationship Between Intuitive Decision Making and Happiness." *European Scientific Journal* (2016); Soosalu, G., S. Henwood, and A. Deo. "Head, Heart, and Gut in Decision Making: Development of a Multiple Brain Preference Questionnaire." *SAGE Journals, mBIT International.* First Published March 18, 2019. doi. org/10.1177/2158244019837439

- A sweating reaction

The next level is defining this manifestation for yourself. We understand it at the language level, but the descriptions and definitions can only take us so far. You need to apply it to make your gut feelings the effective tools they are designed to be. You need to keep your eyes and ears perked for those moments throughout your days.

It could be as simple as a basic exercise, such as listening to different radio stations. Give that a try in the car. Listen to your body as you listen to the radio and switch stations. Notice how your body reacts to the variety—such as classical versus pop.

Do you notice some variation to your state of being? Your breath? This skill set will empower you in life overall and will bring you to the next level—above average—in execution of life decisions, big and small.

Practical Examples

I want to share two examples. One example was a gut feeling in which I felt led toward something, and in the other, I felt led away from something and needed to check in.

The first one was unshakable knowing.

That was a time in my life and healing journey where I had hit a wall, so to speak. The finances were starting to tighten. I was not in a place where I was able to receive my healing in a palpable way. At that time, a person came into my life who had recommended a clinic that specialized in the population with issues similar to mine.

After researching it, I had this unshakable clarity that I needed to go to this clinic; this was what I needed to do. It wasn't a feeling like excitement when your football team wins. It was centered, and I was convinced it was where I needed to go.

It was a five-and-a-half hour drive, and I wasn't able to stay in the car for more than thirty minutes at a time. It was expensive, and our finances were tight. I was going to be there for two weeks. And, I hadn't been apart from my husband for more than a day since the accident. Despite these obstacles, I had a gut feeling and a knowing that was as if I had known all along. As sure as I was that my name was Nicole, God graced me with this knowledge that this was where He was leading me.

I said to my husband, "I need to go to this clinic."

He came back understandably with logistics. *Where was I going to stay? How was I going to eat? I needed to take care of my responsibilities in my hometown.*

I said, "I know, but this is something that we need to do." When we discussed finances, I said, "We're going to raise the money. I will put up a crowdfunding campaign, and we will raise the money."

I spoke confidently. He is a wonderful support, and we took that leap of faith. Within one week, we had a large sum of money. We raised over $10K to send me off to receive this treatment. I will never forget when we hit this goal. I looked at my husband and realized it had happened. We had received this. It was an awesome moment to confirm that visceral knowing, that gut feeling, that God was saying: *This is where you need to go, and I will make a way in this world, right now.*

The second example is what I call *a process involving discernment* and is when you're sensing being led away.

I had seen a variety of specialists through my healing journey. I went to someone who was recommended by another physician. He had high marks on paper and was a great option. I'm sure he is a great doctor. I went into his office, displayed my case, and it was quite evident as we moved forward that we were not a good fit. My questions weren't being answered adequately. I was feeling dismissed. I wasn't receiving a lot of eye contact. These were little things I started to notice. Then, I noticed how the encounter was impacting my visceral knowing—tightness at my neck and jaw for example.

A lot of times you go into situations with no real gut feeling. You figure it out within the setting. Try to keep your emotions out of the equation, being as objective as you can. Take mental notes of how it is going within yourself as well as responses from the other person. It's not always easy, but it is important because you can then take a step back and say: *I don't think this is a good fit.*

You can discern with God within yourself. At first, you can simply take note of the signals and go through the discernment process after. But with time and practice, you will be able to do so in real time.

Of course, that doctor had recommendations for me—followup testing he thought I needed to do, and medications. He had a plan. I walked out respectfully, taking all that and going to God about it. I recognized what that doctor was recommending was not an effective plan for me to follow. God led me to a second medical opinion.

Time and time again, I followed a gut feeling like that one—not to say I was noncompliant with medical recommendations. I went back to the original physician who referred me and asked for a second opinion from a different physician before pursuing that plan of care. We went ahead and did so. Meeting with that second-opinion doctor was an experience in which my gut feeling confirmed he was meant to be a part of my progression through my healing journey. That doctor had vastly different recommendations.

These two experiences were both critical skills for me in shaping the trajectory of healing coming forth. Not only that, but it also resulted in grander understanding and connection with Our Creator and opportunities to celebrate His presence in me, in my life, and in each moment.

Learning to Trust

The essential thing I'll say about trust is: God gave us these gut feelings as an avenue to connect and trust in Him. God is alive and among and within us through the Holy Spirit, thanks to Jesus Christ. While we are absolutely called to be active participants, we also must be driven from a place of trust—trusting God's design. We are designed to partner with our loving Father. The first step is to trust the process.

We are God's design, and we know that God's design is greater than our own understanding. One step at a time, He will reveal truth and drive it home to each of us to suit our own unique way. Then we are called to act accordingly.

Part of trusting God's design is to trust the process. I love listening to birds and birdsong. When I hear birds, it reminds me of this Bible verse.

> *Look at the birds. They don't plant or harvest or store food in barns. Dear Heavenly Father feeds them. And aren't you far more valuable to Him than they are?*
> Matthew 6:26, NLT

Keeping in mind—the birds do not live in their nests all day. They go out into the world to get their food—acting on

God's design. God provides for us all the more as we trust in His source.

We often hear: *Trust in God, trust the process, trust yourself.* If I can share an honest moment about trust, I think it's hard. It's hard to do and it's an intricate process. We are called as children of God to come to understand and live out that trust. When we do, it can be so powerful.

So, how do we do that?

How do we lean in to this discomfort and trust?

My answer: one baby step at a time. My hope is that you can ultimately recognize the power I am giving you. My hope is that, by reading my story, you can ultimately recognize the power that is yours to take.

Remember the practice of listening to different radio stations to see how they impact your feelings?

Take note of how interacting with different people makes you feel within. Pay attention to the little patterns you experience within your body. Then honor them and allow space for such messages to be brought forth so they are a component in your decision making. Bring these messages to your prayer time and conversation with God.

You may start small, or maybe you'll be led in a big way. Either way—you are becoming a holistic, discerning follower of God by letting Him provide for you. You are following His lead, trusting Him.

LEARNING AS YOU GO

It's easier to say: *I need to be given a process. I want to be given the directions of what I need to do. Then, I will be able to do it. Give me the GPS instructions, the map, and I will follow.*

Which is where I have found myself in prayer many a time. But I am repeatedly reminded of God's design. Instead, God reveals to us little by little as we go down the path before us, hand in hand with Him.

His process is simply not designed like a GPS. Believe me, I am all about my workbooks and five-point checklists. I find them helpful. I have developed some. In some parts of life, that is the way it works.

But these are tools; they are not the overarching way. Lists are like having road signs, while God's design is the entire journey. What we are learning about, what we are leaning in to, is God's design. God has it set up in a way too intricate for a checklist, and much grander than a series of goals. His design is infinite, all encompassing, and abundant. Because of this, we are called to do three things: Respect/celebrate the individual nature of your life, mind, body and soul; connect with God regularly to discern the way to pursue the growth

He is leading you toward; and embrace the process in pursuit of it including His supernatural grace.

Individuality

You and I are unique persons. While we have similarities and consistencies in our designs, we are so intricate that within those consistencies are components unique to you and components unique to me. This is part of the reason why this process cannot be a five-point handbook or checklist. That is not how God designed it.

Instead, I feel God encouraging us to lean in to that individuality, recognize biblical truths, and come to Him where He is working in our lives. Together with God we will find a way to pursue what is before us.

Wayne Dyer speaks on this referencing the power of the great I AM through the story of Moses and the burning bush.[12]

In the book of Exodus, God speaks to Moses through a bush that appears to be burning but is not consumed by flames. (Exodus 3:1–17) God tells Moses what he wants Moses to do—or what to pursue next in his life's journey—and empowers him, saying *"I will be with you."* Dyer reviews—"I AM that I Am is the name of God. And every time you

---

12 Dyer, Wayne. "Mastering the Art of Manifesting." *Wanderlust's SpeakEasy Conference* (Squaw Valley, CA, July 2012). YouTube Video. youtube.com/watch?v=zNrEFpkgWQo

use the phrase 'I am' you are using the name of God. So, it is important that we utilize such a phrase to proclaim the power and healing love in our lives. Affirmations are a type of practice of this—I am healed, I am whole, I am well."

Wayne references the book of Joel where it is written, "Let the weak say I am strong." (Joel 3:10) These are very powerful and practical tools to partner with God and follow His lead or his call for our lives to come from a place of abundance.

Discernment

After gut feelings, *discernment* is the second component to learn. Discernment is listening to God.

I grew up in the church. I had never heard the word *discernment* until I started down this healing journey. I have come to find I am not alone in this experience. Discernment has been a huge piece of this practical application because it is the way I hear how God is moving in my life.

Discernment has caused a big leap in my ability to reach what is in front of me, with God, in and throughout my day. Prior to understanding and getting in touch with discernment, talking to or connecting with God was something I did in church groups: class, at church itself, or afterward at a prayer time.

Living my day, it was like I have that life too. But there was no cohesion. It was like I had separate parts of my life. While

I had faith in Him absolutely, my ability to feel communion with Him was not nearly to the level it was once I understood how to discern.

To be clear, discernment is not a fleeting emotion or even a passionate emotion. It is not a state of contentment or uncertainty. Discernment speaks over and above these states. In the preface to the late Henri Nouwen's book, *Discernment: Reading the Signs of Daily Life,* Robert A. Jonas explains Nouwen's take on Christian discernment:

> Discernment is not the same as decision making. Reaching a decision can be straightforward: we consider our goals and options; maybe we list the pros and cons of each possible choice; and then we choose the action that meets our goal most effectively. Discernment, on the other hand, is about listening and responding to that place within us where our deepest desires align with God's desire.[13]

And Henri Nouwen himself wrote, "Discernment is a life of listening to a deeper sound and marching to a different beat, a life in which we become 'all ears.' "[14]

---

13 Christensen, Michael J. and Rebecca J. Laird. Preface to *Discernment: Reading the Signs of Daily Life* by Nouwen. HarperCollins, 2013. XV.

14 Nouwen, Henri. *Discernment: Reading the Signs of Daily Life.* HarperCollins, 2013. 5.

We are challenged to lean in to this beat and learn how to respond in kind.

Here's an example: I would pray to God and ask for prayer during these structured prayer times or in church itself. "God heal me." Not a bad prayer. Sometimes it would be an involved hands on prayer but no healing would be received. But two things were revealed to me: the first was my action—I would go out of that time and continue with my patterns that were rooted in sickness. Like, I would get a nudge to write this book and I'd reply to God, "I can no longer read," or I would get a nudge to pray for someone else and I would reply, "I have nothing to offer."

I came to understand that while God can and does provide such abundance and miraculous acts including healing, it is our responsibility to adjust and live it out in turn.

The second thing is the way I was praying—"God heal me." That word choice reflects how my mind is focused not on God's healing but my need to be healed. In other words —in sickness. Charles Capps, the author of *The Tongue: A Creative Force (1976)*, does a beautiful deep dive into the power of word choice. How we ask to be led will influence how we will hear the voice of God.

When I began to use such a tool and changed my prayers with God as the focal point, I was brought to a new level. So, instead of praying, "God, heal me," I began to pray things like, "God, you are the Alpha and the Omega," "You are the grand physician," and, "You promise complete healing in the name of Jesus."

Grace

"Grace: Freely given, unmerited favor and love of God. Influence or spirit of God operating in humans to regenerate and put His strength in them." (dictionary.com)

I love grace. God's grace is never-ending. We understand that we have God's grace, which is powerful and important because we are learning as we go. You are going to make mistakes; they are part of the learning process. If you are not making mistakes, you are not delving into this process completely.

Recognizing God's grace is available to us and then receiving it is critical. Only when we make mistakes and let God's grace cover us are we genuinely open to learning and being shaped by that learning process. And through His grace, we have the strength to make it through our learning and become better for it.

While we are called to openly receive God's grace, we also need to have grace for ourselves. For example, it's okay that we make a mistake. When I make a mistake, it can really rock me, particularly if there are negative consequences. What I have come to understand is I need to prayerfully come to being okay that I did something that missed the mark of God's leading or my hopes. I need to do so coming from a place of complete love, connected with God's love for us so we can be renewed and delve deeper into partnering with Him.

As soon as we do that completely, we take the shame away from the mistake. We are able to learn from it and grow. We really do become better for it. We need to lean in to it, and we should do so completely in order to truly receive grace in its fullness.

Once we are able to do this, a third facet is grace for others. Every single person we come across in our life is human. They have been, just like you and I have been, in their own life. They are also created in the image of God. For me, giving others grace is a pathway to forgive, and then learn from the experience. It builds upon our learning about this process as a whole.

> *For if, by the trespass of the one man, death reigned through that one man, how much more will those who receive God's abundant provision of grace and of the gift of righteousness reign in life through the one man, Jesus Christ!*
> Romans 5:17, NIV

One of the hardest lessons I have had on this journey has been to receive something as beautifully powerful as God's grace so freely given. I was completely wrapped up in identifying with the need to earn this grace. I would talk the talk no problem, but when it came to my quiet moments, I felt so unworthy that I deeply struggled with even fathoming that I could access such a gift.

I would often say, "I will never ever be able to do enough. No matter what I do, it's never enough; it's never right. I am not getting it—how am I supposed to connect with my Creator when I can't seem to do anything right?"

The answer came as clear as day. You're not supposed to earn it. This isn't a works thing. This is a gift because you are deeply and unconditionally loved. So, all that you do is to be met with that love and grace. That is God's design.

PROCESSES

This section is like a Cliff Notes version of what is involved in living out how God is leading you. I share some critical components about how to live following God's lead. Again, it is an extremely dynamic process. So, while this is not an extensive list, I do believe that the core components outlined here are excellent places to start.

Community

After my injury, my community began to crumble. Over the year that was to follow, I was getting worse and worse and people don't want to hear about that. One by one, neighbors, acquaintances, friends, and even family fell away. This was devastating at the time. I felt abandoned and like I was burdening my husband. But I now thank God for the power of forgiveness and the way he uses all things for His good.

Once I forgave, I slowly became open to connecting with others again. As I connected with my community, I came to see how I was forever changed and maintaining that old community was no longer appropriate. They were looking to connect with the Nicole prior to the injury. Looking to have me *back*.

I remember one of the last days I went to our church at the time, a church friend came up to me and put her hand on my shoulder asking, "How are you doing?" I gave her the basic update, that I still had three different therapies I was doing and was pursuing different diet changes and specialists.

She replied, "Do you think you will ever be able to make it back to where you were?" I remember smiling at her, replying, "I will never be the same."

That was the moment for me—I realized that while I needed to connect with others in a variety of ways, I was no longer to do so in the community I knew and loved. A large number of them could not see me for where I was in my journey. They were looking to connect with someone who, in a manner of speaking, was no longer there. My spiritual depth and physical abilities had drastically changed in short order. This season had come to its end and a new one was beginning.

As human beings, we are meant to participate and live in and among the community. It can be challenging, particularly when you have experienced a major health change in your life. Sometimes what your community looks like will change. That change can be a hard reality.

Emotional healing may need to happen to welcome a change in the makeup of your community. Whether you are in a place where you need to reach out and build your community, or maybe rebuild it, it is vital in moving forward through this process.

There is no doubt in my mind we are called to have a community. It is where God can speak and work. A community keeps you well rounded, open, grounded, and challenged. Within your community, certain types of people are necessary.

One type of person is the one who plays a supportive role. We need somebody in our life who supports us. A second person is a mentor, someone we can turn to and receive their wisdom, life experience, and their point of view. Others may include people who challenge you, who bring you growth, who empathize with you, or who bring fun into your day.

Embrace the changing tides of your community. For it is through our willingness to receive God's grace, forgive, heal, and connect with others that we can experience the fullness of life. And in so experiencing, we are properly positioned to all that God longs to gift us.

Prayer

> *Very early in the morning, while it was still dark,*
> *Jesus got up, left the house and went off to a solitary*
> *place, where he prayed.*
> Mark 1:35, NIV

Prayer is communication with God. Prayer time, as modeled by Jesus, is simply quiet time to commune with God.

Pastor Brian Forrester spoke on the topic of how to pray in his sermon at All Nations Church on February 3, 2019. He outlined three main components to the structure of prayer time with God.[15]

Worship: Set an intention of praise. This intention could be with words, through body language, or maybe turning on a certain kind of music or singing.

Praying: Communicating with God. He recommends starting with the ACTS model.

ACTS stands for:

- Adoration, claiming how awesome God is
- Confession, an opportunity to bring to God anything weighing on your heart
- Thanksgiving, *Thank God!*
- Supplication, requests to God

---

15 The author was present at this service: All Nations Church, 853 Cloverleaf Lane, Newport News, Virginia.

Scripture: Read from the Bible as some component of this time. As for choosing a version, he recommends picking the version that speaks to you the most or the one you understand easily.

What's great about our technology today is that you can download the Bible onto your smartphone for free and try out different translations before purchasing a Bible.

So now that we know what to do, we can explore how to do it. Journaling, prayer walks, and time with God are all examples of how we can be active participants in God's movements. Whether it is in the format of a journal—writing a letter, a written conversation, or bulleted list format—or something more active where you are walking and talking to God, intentionally put aside a practice in the routine of your day, every day as fits your own style.

When it comes to healing, talk to God about it.

If you feel you need direction, there are four things you can do:

1. Turn to the back of the Bible and look up scripture under the category of *healing*. Read one.

2. Talk to God. Ask Him to reveal what in your life needs healing.

3. Write down what comes.

4. Ask God: *What is most critical or the first thing to tackle here?*

We do our discernment practice, wait, and hear. We connect with Him and receive His love and leading. It's vital you understand this is a partnership with the Creator of the world, our savior.

It's going to happen in a variety of ways. It won't necessarily happen the same way every time. We can participate in this communication time with him differently throughout our days.

Some activities may include:

- Journaling
- Prayer walks
- Painting or art
- Singing or playing music
- Building
- Running
- Study

We can turn to the Bible and read that immediate, miraculous healing are part of how God works. It's not necessarily going to be instantaneous. Sometimes, we need to walk alongside Him in this process, if you will, because it is only from this foundation of prayer that we can then move forward confidently in pursuit of complete healing in Jesus' name.

Research, Document, Prepare, and Execute

God has already promised healing is within you. Use these components—prayer, discernment, and community—to identify how He is leading you to bring forth that healing. You need to recognize you have what God is longing to bring forth in you. You need to listen for how He is going to execute it. Then, you need to take a leap of faith.

Go ahead and move.

Research and Document. Verify what you are thinking by collecting the details of the topic before you. Having identified what God is leading you toward, document it. Start a log. Start a Word document. Start a Google document. Create something in a simple and accessible format so you have information to refer to.

This step sets you up for success as you pursue what is before you. As the process progresses and the layers build, outside forces can threaten your fervency. They can challenge your assurance that you know the objective in front of you and cloud your judgment. With written documentation, however, you have the words God spoke to you, scripture, and whatever other format, context, or resources brought you to this decision.

Preparation. For example, let's say you have researched a doctor's office. Your research all rings true to how your gut is feeling, how God is leading you. Prepare for this appointment. You can find details of how to do that in the Next Steps section of this book. You should walk into these appointments well-read. It can feel like a high-pressure situation, so you want to set yourself up for success. Write down your core thoughts, questions, future thoughts, and things of this nature.

How to Prepare for an Appointment

- Prepare your heart: Recognize the place your heart is in when approaching this appointment slot—Are you nervous? Anxious? Excited? Grounded? Assured?

- Prepare your mind: Are your thoughts coming from a place of abundance or lack? Skeptic or open-minded?

- Prepare your knowledge base: Find three reputable sources that support this decision, and three that do not. Empower yourself to know both sides of the argument. For example, I went into an acupuncture appointment with the understanding of peer-reviewed articles supporting and not supporting an intervention for treatment of headaches.

- Prepare your action: Write down your core thoughts, questions, and curiosities. This will allow you to maximize your efficiency during the appointment.

Execution. You must go to the appointment. Call and make the appointment as soon as you recognize this is your path.

There may be a waiting period, which varies in length. This time is when you can do more preparation.

I can remember once being led to a neurologist whose wait list was three months long, an hour and a half away, and out of network. Two years later, I made the appointment. This was after having tried three other neurologists who were in-network and in town. While I don't regret this course—as I can now pass it on to others—I certainly recognize that two years is a whole lot longer than three months to wait. Make the appointment—you can figure out logistics after. Not to mention, it is often easier to reschedule than to start from scratch!

The execution is two-pronged. The first prong is making the appointment and the second is walking into the appointment. I can personally attest to making an appointment, and when my nerves got the best of me, I was unable to go. I ended up canceling. I can personally attest to scheduling an appointment, driving to the parking lot, and then becoming so nervous and overwhelmed that I couldn't move. I remember once feeling frozen in the driver's seat, my hands sweating and shaking, tears running down my face. I knew I needed help and that this was where I was led to get it—but I could not physically move. I ended up canceling and rescheduling twice.

At that point, I went back to grace and worked through my nerves. I attempted to execute again. I affirmed it was what

I needed to do as the next step in the process. So, I needed to try again. In those cases, community played a big role. In this instance, I was ultimately able to walk through the doors when I had my husband at my side. I had asked him to simply be there with me, to take a supportive role, holding me accountable and reminding me of unconditional love. You need to figure out how to make it happen.

Who in your tribe could take that role for you?

How can you find ways to connect to Our God and walk through those proverbial doors?

Reflect. After executing, you celebrate that leap of faith and all involved. Yay! You did it! Bask in the afterglow. Then, you reflect on the experience and information received. Bring components of it to God as you feel led. Discern how you are called to move forward.

In my neurologist example, the appointment was out of town. If this is the case, you write out all the logistics involved. You walk through that. Again, you research, document, prepare, and execute within each of those steps as well. Move and repeat.

You also want to create a central place to keep all these documents and copies of your own medical records, which you may obtain with a simple ask at the end of the appointment. They don't offer them willingly most of the time, so you will have to ask. When I first started I had a little red binder with all of my documents. While it can still be helpful to have hard copies, I now find most offices are open to electronic format, and I now have all of my personal health records in the cloud.

This all sets you up for success in executing how God is creating with you.

CHAPTER FIVE

Encouraging and Empowering: How to Use This Framework

COMMITMENT

We now have tools and resources. In addition, it's critical to create a practice that assists us in applying that knowledge in a way that yields results.

> *Let us hold tightly without wavering to the hope we affirm so God can be trusted to keep His promise.*
> Hebrews 10:23, NLT

This is my go-to verse when I am in a place in which my commitment is being challenged. As we pursue this framework, my hope is that a verse like this will always be a guiding light to you. God means what He says. He tells us what He promises. Our hope in such a source is unrelenting.

For God's fulfillment for His children is through Christ, therefore, we must set ourselves up for successful execution as we partner with Him. There are three core components I found essential to maintain my tight hold on hope. They are *spiritual practice, commitment,* and *goals.*

Spiritual Practice

To review, we have talked about the components of our framework, such as having the desire for healing. We have worked on knowledge of that healing and faith in the healing. Now it's time to talk about spiritual action. If we regard Jesus as our model, a good resource to turn to, I want to examine his spiritual actions when he was flesh here on Earth.

A spiritual action is a practice in which you can connect with your spiritual self. I was led to two main practices that are specifically designed to help us do this. The first one is the practice of going off alone to pray. It's written many times that was a practice of Jesus.

Read:

- Matthew 14:13, 14:23
- Mark 1:35, Mark 3:13
- Mark 14:32
- Luke 5:16, 9:1

It's time to put in place some of the practices we outlined earlier: prayer walks, journaling, art, meditation, or something of a similar nature. Be sure to set an amount of time aside consistently each day for Christ. There are a lot of studies about how much time is beneficial. We will delve into specifics of that later.

Suffice it to say, you need to start somewhere. Start with one minute if that's what you need to do. You just need to start. You set yourself up for success with commitment.

To assist in this, give yourself a schedule that includes:

- The place
- Time of day
- Amount of time
- Materials

For example, you might commit yourself to one minute in the morning at the foot of your bed to read the daily Bible verse on your app for one week. Then, build from this practice when you feel ready. During the second week, you might find you can read more like two minutes, then five, then seven, then ten. Or maybe you add a journal or adjust the location.

The goal is not the amount of time. The goal is consistent intention every day. A plan for this time is good to reference if you are feeling uncertain or lost. While there are many resources within a simple internet search, I encourage you to turn back to our conversation in the Processes heading under the Prayer section in Chapter Four, recommended by Pastor Brian Forrester.

The second thing is to weave what you receive in that quiet alone prayer time into your daily moments. As you are living out your day, find a way to weave in those truths.

As Pastor Rick Warren says, "The habit of 'praying without ceasing' (from 1 Thessalonians 5:17) means conversing with God while shopping, driving, working, or performing any other everyday task. . . . Everything you do can be spending time with God if He is invited to be a part of it and you stay aware of His presence."[16]

Here are a few quick ideas I found beneficial.

One was creating a *mantra*. A mantra is a short sentence that encompasses the core of what you received in your spirit. All you do with a mantra is repeat this quiet phrase to yourself throughout the day.

Some examples:

- *Be still and know that I am God.*
- *Jesus Christ, have mercy on me.*
- *I am Yours and You are mine.*

What is your mantra in this season?

_____

16 Warren, Rick. "Be in Constant Communion with God—Daily Hope with Rick Warren." February 16, 2019. Viewed on March 21, 2020. oneplace.com/ministries/daily-hope/read/devotionals/daily-hope-with-rick-warren/be-in-constant-communion-with-god-daily-hope-with-rick-warren-february-16-2019-11805142.html

What phrase encompasses God's movement with your spirit?

A second idea is placing a quote where you can see it often. Find words that motivate your spirit and reconnect you to a spiritual truth moment. I placed mine on the dashboard of my car. I found it helpful because it was a concrete representation of what I wanted to weave into my daily life.

The one on my dashboard was given to me in God's perfect timing, exactly when I needed it:

> *Visualize this thing you want. See it, feel it, believe*
> *in it. Make your mental blueprint and begin.*
> ~ Robert Collier

This quote provided me assurance in moments that tested my faith. Faith in the process of God's design. This gave me action items to use in turning to God and believing in His healing hand. It allowed me to honor the fact that this is my mental blueprint, so adjustments are inevitable. Blueprints in construction are great—they provide significant information and data for execution, but they are not the building.

My husband worked in construction for a time, and I can remember him working on this one job site that gave them so much trouble. The team was constantly adjusting how to build the building given the blueprints laid out for them. Time and time again, they were needing to make adaptations to the original blueprint in order to execute the plan in a way that the building would be structurally sound. I remember at one point, they were so frustrated with attempting to follow the original blueprints, that one team member threw the blueprints out of the window of his moving vehicle!

What a beautiful metaphor for our lives and healing journeys! Your blueprint is a great framework—but adjust it and draft up new blueprints when you find execution is requiring adaptations to the original plan.

Another idea is finding music or entertainment that supports a spiritual connection. The background image on your phone and computer can represent that as well. Be creative; think outside the box.

Go ahead, and name your own practice now. Give yourself something that is going to give you real-time access to our Heavenly Father in your day.

Outline the core components of your *alone time*—place, time of day, amount of time, materials. And commit to trying one mantra and one visual reminder. It's not simply one idea or task that is your key to connect spiritually. You need to create an overall supportive environment to grow your spiritual practice.

Committing to Yourself, and in Turn, to Your Savior

Let's take a moment to think about the cross and God's commitment to us—what Jesus did for us in being crucified, dying, and rising again. He took all our sin—brokenness, wounds, sickness, disease—to the cross and buried it forever, providing a new way. When Jesus rose again, he shared that we are now his hands and feet by God's design.

That models God's commitment to me, and I recognize my humanness and what I am facing. If I am his vessel now, and my body is God's temple now, it's up to me to show up, to do my part, and participate. God leads with unwavering faith in me, and I find commitment to myself is much more palatable when I think of it in terms of a grander purpose.

> *Or do you not know that your body is a temple of the Holy Spirit within you, whom you have from God? You are not your own, for you were bought with a price. So glorify God in your body.*
> 1 Corinthians 6: 19–20 ESV

I know I need to renew my commitment when I see patterns of self-destruction. Usually, I am connecting only to myself, and then I feel really small. Doubts start to come in. I feel like it doesn't matter. Excuses start to creep in.

It isn't enough to *say* I am committing to myself because it is best for me. I need to *know* I am committed to something bigger than myself—to God's grander design that He's manifesting through me. Because He works through me, I do not need to be self-reliant, sustained by my own strength and strong will. I rely on God's strength and God's will.

Giving Yourself Goals

It is good for workers to have an appetite. An
empty stomach drives them on.

Proverbs 16:26, NLT

The clinical field loves goals, action items, and measured progress toward them. As a speech therapist clinician, I bought in to this early on, and one could say structuring life according to goals is in my psyche, how I view life. But there've been countless times when I gave myself goals, action items to achieve them, timelines and deadlines, and reward systems, and failed to execute. Talk about discouraging!

There was plenty to fuel the flames of doubt and rejection in those moments. Fear and despair come in instantly. What happened? I was committed, felt passionate, and sensed this plan was something God longed for in my life. The confusion led me to understand I needed to talk to God about it.

In this context, I came to understand God wanted me to use goals a bit differently. A goal, in His plan, is not meant to be the central focus. The central focus is to keep my eyes on how He leads me. The goal is meant to be like a trail marker along the healing journey. That is all. The focus is to be kept on Him.

Stephen Covey offers a wonderful analogy:

> Think about taking a trip on an airplane. Before taking off, the pilot has a very clear destination

in mind, which hopefully coincides with yours, and a flight plan to get there. The plane takes off at the appointed hour toward that predetermined destination. But in fact, the plane is off course at least 90 percent of the time. Weather conditions, turbulence, and other factors cause it to get off track. However, feedback is given to the pilot constantly, who then makes course corrections and keeps coming back to the exact flight plan, bringing the plane back on course. And often, the plane arrives at the destination on time. It's amazing. Think of it. Leaving on time, arriving on time, but off course 90 percent of the time.[17]

God showed me this is how goals are meant to be used. You can develop them simply by having a big one and then giving yourself action items to reach this larger goal. Within the action item, you may need to develop smaller, short-term goals, all functioning as guideposts—not necessarily as accomplishments to earn a gold star every step of the way. Missing a step on the way is not a big deal because that's not the point. The point is to keep your gaze toward Jesus Christ.

For specifics on how to develop a goal-driven plan—I recommend reading Chapter 3 of Tommy Newberry's 2007 book, *Success Is Not an Accident.*

---

17 Covey, Stephen R. *How to Develop Your Personal Mission Statement.* Grand Harbor Press, 2013.

Scripture gives us a famously powerful example in Matthew 14: 28–31 (NLT) after the disciples have seen Jesus walking on the water:

> Then Peter called to him, 'Lord if it's really you, tell me to come to you, walking on the water.' 'Yes, come,' Jesus said. So Peter went over the side of the boat and walked on the water toward Jesus. But when he saw the strong wind and waves, he was terrified and began to sink. 'Save me, Lord!' he shouted. Jesus immediately reached out and grabbed him.

If it is when Peter looks to the wind and the waves that he becomes fearful and begins to sink, then I believe his gaze must have been on Jesus when he, too, was walking on water. And this is my point: when we keep Jesus as our central focus, He faithfully guides our steps. It is in those moments that we have access to the peace that transcends all understanding and find ourselves living out things that we never thought possible. It is when we shift to looking at the wind and waves that we find we are victims to our fears.

Without fail, when I'm struggling in this area, God helps me see that my gaze—my intention, my motivation, the driving force to achievement—has shifted. Coming back to Him leads us to claim Him as our source of strength and view goals simply as guideposts as we follow God's lead, taking His hand and gazing at His intention, trusting His design as we pursue the path before us. Trusting and knowing that He is using all things for good. Accepting the reality of missing a goal here and there—each and every goal is simply a format to chart out moving into uncharted territory.

When in this state, I find my goals become bigger than I would have imagined. My passion for attainment is unshakable. And often I find myself passively adjusting and problem solving as I pursue the path before me. Now we are functioning in flow with His design.

In flow with our God is an abstract state of being that is difficult to put into words. Suffice it to say that when we reach this place, we are functioning from a place where self-preservation, criticism, and fear are finally out of the way. We feel connected at our core to our creator and discern in real time. This is when many sub-goals might come under the grand objective of complete healing in Jesus's name. And it is in such a state that complete self-acceptance and forgiveness can come in. It is here that we can celebrate our oneness with our Heavenly Father, the power within, and gain perspective.

GIVING YOURSELF GRACE

> *Timothy, my dear son, be strong through the grace*
> *that God gives you in Christ Jesus.*
> 2 Timothy 2:1, NLV

That affirms the truth that it's God at work, and we simply receive what God is doing in our lives. We are strong because of Him, through His grace. Grace is more than forgiveness. There is forgiveness in grace. It's also love and passion, a renewal. It's intimate.

One of my favorite parts about this verse is it talks about the power of grace. If it's coming from the Creator of all things, I guess we shouldn't be surprised. I don't think *power* is necessarily what we think of when we think of grace. To be empowered gives ourselves a way to receive that kind of grace openly and completely. We're designed for grace and God wants it in our lives.

The Father-Son Parable

I heard a wonderful story once by a pastor, Art Thomas.[18] He is a pastor known for preaching about healing. This parable was of a father and his little boy. In the corner of the backyard was a tree where the father wanted to build a tree house he and his son could enjoy together. He had just come home from the hardware store with all the supplies needed to build a treehouse for he and his son to enjoy together.

He drove the truck as close as he could to the tree, but needed to walk the supplies across the yard a bit to reach the tree. He

---

18 Thomas, Art. "Effortless Healing." *Art Thomas Ministries,* February 13, 2015. Viewed on March 29, 2020 at youtube.com/watch?v=cjwvJ2cZ7HA

gathered about four pieces of lumber, hoisted them on his shoulder, and began the trek toward the tree.

The son ran up alongside him and was so excited. "Can I help you?"

The father stopped walking and looked at him. He realized the whole point of building this playhouse was so he and his son could enjoy time together. He put the two-by-fours down on the ground and said to his son, "Come help me."

The son picked up part of one board, and the father picked up the other. At the little-boy speed of tiny little steps, they walked this board all the way to the tree. They did it again. They went back to the truck, picked out a board, and walked. The father couldn't complete this process as quickly as doing it with his own two hands. But, he was enjoying it because he was working with his child.

For me, that is an excellent metaphor of God working this progressive process with His child. We make a commitment to partner with Him, build with Him, and execute as best as we are able every day. We trust that each step of the way is a part of God's grander intention, and we cherish the truth that He is pleased to execute it at our pace.

It's a beautiful metaphor for how God is committed to us, loves us, and simply enjoys co-creating with us. In doing so, He allows us to participate with the process of creation.

Because we are human, there will be drops, mismanagement, or mismeasurement as we build together.

It requires a big shift in our mental capacity to recognize mistakes are part of how this co-creation works, a part of the design.

It can be freeing to say: *Okay, let me take a moment to go to God and check in with myself and be okay with this thing I am seeing as a mistake.*

Give yourself grace. Receive His grace.

The Road Is Not Straight

When we see point A and point B, we want to draw a straight line to move from one to the other. That simply is not life. Often, it doesn't work out that way. Our emotions can be charged when we face the reality of the not-straight road. We may feel frustration about a detour on the way to our destination; we feel unable to go about traveling in the way we had envisioned. We might experience anger or disappointment.

Have you been unable to travel down a road in the convenience you had envisioned because of your own doing?

I once got a flat tire on my way home from work. Why? Because I'd been driving on bald tires for a little too long. Then *bump!* One day the front passenger tire simply gave.

This realization led to another whole layer of emotions: guilt, shame, self-deprecation, and so on.

When considering the road before us, we can glean some insight from these metaphorical parallels. We may hold our God-given destination in mind on our way down the road to pursue it, but let's keep in mind we do not know the way like our Lord. This is particularly important to keep in mind when the road takes a turn that feels like it was your own doing—like my flat tire.

Let's not let those emotions that flood the situation, staring us in the face, take over. Instead, let us recognize the situation, honor the emotions, and check in with our source. It is so critical to check in with God to recognize you have access to this powerful grace to remember that you are committed to the Creator of all things so you don't get derailed!

A piece of scripture that helps me check in and guide myself when I am in these moments is Isaiah 40:28–31, (NLT):

> *Have you never heard? Have you never understood? The Lord is the everlasting God, the Creator of all the Earth. He never grows weak or weary. No one can measure the depth of His understanding. He gives power to the weak and strength to the powerless. Even the useful become weak and tired, and young men will fall in exhaustion. But those who trust in the Lord will find new strength. They will soar high on wings like eagles. They will run and not grow weary. They will walk and not faint.*

You see how God speaks to us?

God never grows weak. All humans—even the skilled and the young—grow weak. But God gives in such a way His child soars, even in their weakness. His design is such that as we welcome His provision, He joyfully provides His power and His strength. We travel with Him as partners who continue the journey ahead as one unstoppable being.

My Go-To Practices for Giving Myself Grace

We have reviewed what God's grace is, how and why God designed it, and what its role is in the context of our healing journey. Now, let's discuss how to access it.

The first step is to recognize the need to access it. To accomplish this, you must take a step back from viewing life through your own lens. You need to turn within in a nonjudgmental way so you can recognize the need to receive grace.

Next, you must make this need a priority and simply act. If you're able to do it in the moment, that's preferred. But, if you need to set time aside for later, that's fine too. I find the longer the situation festers, the longer I have to work to receive grace. Addressing it quickly prevents the roots from digging deeper into me.

So, what is this *receiving grace* practice?

It can be executed in many different ways. The main purpose is to provide a conduit to connect with God and His unending grace. The first action in all grace practices is to claim this time to welcome God in all His beauty and grace.

For a scripture-based grace practice, I recommend the following:

1. Write down the situation in which you need grace.

2. Leave it on the paper.

3. Find a scripture like the one we reviewed from Isaiah 40. An easy Google search will do or look in the back of a bible under *grace*.

4. Write down what jumps out in the passage. Typically, it is a verse or so.

5. Explore the relationship between the scripture and your situation.

6. Ask God to help you release what you are holding on to and fill your heart with grace, light, and love.

I also have a mantra-based practice. For this one, I create a simple mantra I repeat to myself for a set amount of time or set activity.

It could be simple:

- *Thank You for grace.*

- *I welcome Your grace, God.*

- *Forgive me for ___.*

I make that mantra my inner monologue throughout the time frame. If and when my mind inevitably wanders, I simply bring it back to the mantra. Sometimes I make a note of what I'm wondering about quickly and then return to the mantra. Again, I take note of ways God has helped me release and be forgiven.

Visualization is another style of practice. I encourage you to explore it. The point is to visualize in a way that effectively connects your soul to our Creator's grace. You choose an abstract visualization of colors or mist. Your vision could be an image like watching a movie or having a conversation with Jesus—or anywhere in between. This is a fun one to explore.

Once in a while, you may find it helpful to discuss the call on your heart for God's grace with a close spiritual friend or confidant. I recommend reserving this one for after you've tried a couple of practices during your *you and God* time. God has graciously created us to be a community connected in love and grace. Let's receive that gift and use it.

For by God's design, we pursue this journey with Him in our humanness. Humanness is imperfect and at the same time, God's beauty is amplified in imperfection. We will inevitably have moments in our lives that we view as mistakes, detours on our journeys, or blockades to our paths.

But what if, through His grace, we are living out His ultimate perfection?

Grace is critical here for so many reasons! Some of them are for our ultimate ability to grow deeper in our connection with our savior, for understanding of our lives, and for ultimately receiving the provision of complete healing. I challenge you to put down the text and take a moment to thank our Creator for His gift of grace and receive it in all its glory! You are His child, designed in His image, and designed to live connected to Him and His grace.

> *For by grace you have been saved, through faith.*
> *And this is not your own doing; it is the gift of God,*
> *not a result of works, so that no one may boast.*
> Ephesians 2:8–9, ESV

FORMING NEW HABITS

A habit is an action we do without using a lot of brainpower. When we have habits that are life-giving, assist in our ability to receive God in our life, and bring healing forth in our bodies, we have amazingly powerful tools for success.

Research About Habit Building

In a study published in the *European Journal of Social Psychology*, group members chose one of three behaviors to create a new habit around—drinking, eating, or exercising.

The results of the study were that half the group did not perform the desired behavior consistently enough to achieve habit status.[19]

However, sixty-six days was the median time required to develop a new habit. Consistent practice resulted in better mastery of the target habit over a shorter amount of time. A more complex activity, such as exercise, took a little bit longer. In this study, researchers found it would take one-and-a-half times more effort to achieve a complex habit than the simpler goals of establishing new eating or drinking habits.

Other people offer twenty-one or thirty days as a time frame. I have found this sixty-six-day time frame is how my body, mind, soul weaves a new habit into my life. When discussing this study, Dr. Caroline Leaf teaches that a person needs to dedicate about seven to ten minutes a day to the new practice.[20]

Personally, I encourage choosing whatever will get you started. If it needs to be one minute, then let it be one minute. Recognize that once that is palatable, you will build up from

19 Lally, Phillippa, et. al. "How Habits Are Formed: Modelling Habit Formation in the Real World." *European Journal of Social Psychology.* 16 July 2009. doi: 10.1002/ejsp.674

20 Virkler, Mark. "How Long Does It Take to Create a New Habit?" *XP.* 2018. Retrieved from xpmedia.com/article/18054

there to reach the seven- to ten-minute range. Once you achieve that amount of time, you begin the sixty-six days.

Let's take our receiving grace practice as an example. We set our intention to use this practice in our spiritual life for sixty-six days. We then take a calendar or personal schedule and count out sixty-six days, making a note on the day of completion. We then commit to executing the practice in whatever ways and amounts of time daily are speaking to us.

Then we execute it, keeping in mind what we've discussed earlier about this being a conduit to grow closer to God.

The pattern may work out like this:

- Excitement to do it
- Difficulty doing it
- Forgetting to do it
- Bringing yourself back to doing it
- Shocked when you have had the intentional practice for sixty-six days
- Shocked when it becomes part of your life
- Discover it's a habit you use without much thought— like a cup to pour water into when thirsty

So, let's give it a try! Perhaps you can take our one-minute, get-started time frame right now and try the mantra rooted in God's grace. Congratulations—you have successfully begun a life-changing habit!

Holding Yourself Accountable

There will be bumps in the road. That is simply how it works. It's up to you to decide how these bumps influence your choices, your behavior, and how you live out your days. You need to be accountable to yourself.

Keep in mind, I share these tools to assist you in keeping your gaze on the glory God's willing for you to receive in your life.

One simple suggestion is to talk to someone you trust about what you are trying to form, this new habit. Once you have an ear and a mouth outside your own, you will feel the difference.

Another guidepost is a calendar. This is the place for that gold star. Give yourself a gold star on the days you achieve these new habits. You can keep track of how much time has passed. You also need to honor days you missed. Allow them to simply be, and then pick up and continue. Think of our airplane being off the charted course 90 percent of the time! And remember, it's about having tools that help guide your adjustment to grow in your ability to keep Jesus as your central focus.

Allow for rest. Do not give yourself so much to do that you feel you cannot keep up. Rest is responsibly honoring what your body needs. Mistakes may happen; it's human nature. So, again, do not let that become a roadblock. Ask God to help you use mistakes for His glorious design to shape the path before you.

Once you're at the end of your sixty-six days, you'll look back and feel as though time went by quickly.

Celebrate the possibility before you to form life-giving habits while partnering with our Heavenly Father. This is life-changing in such a way I feel the possibilities are endless!

Review the Commitment

> *Let us not become weary in doing good, for at the*
> *proper time, we will reap a harvest if we do not*
> *give up.*
>
> Galatians 6:9, NIV

This verse of scripture is a beautiful piece encouraging commitment, particularly when we are in the throes of trying to form a good habit. I think we need to see opportunities to reconnect with the promise that God is committed to each of us—you and me. Galatians gives you a nice reminder that this commitment is something you are building with Him.

It's a long-term goal of sorts. "For at the proper time, we will reap a harvest if we do not give up." You and I are like farmers tending their crops. It is worth the commitment so that we can receive the bounty—what the Bible often calls *the fruits*—of our labor. And we do so, trusting in the timing of the process, the time frame our Creator has designed.

If you do have moments of feeling weary, remember the result is in God's hands. You are partnering with Him and carry the promise of harvest from He who gives abundantly. This reminder should reconnect you to the core of what this journey is all about: connection with your Heavenly Father, he who never grows weak or weary. He whose goodness is beyond understanding and whose plans for you are not of evil but of good and prosperity. (Jeremiah 29:11)

He loves you unconditionally and is devoted to you forever and always. One of His deepest longings is for a deeper connection with you. He delights in building this together.

Conclusion

Dear brothers and sisters, one final thing. Fix your
thoughts on what is true, and honorable, and right,
and pure, and lovely, and admirable. Think about
things that are excellent and worthy of praise.
                                        Philippians 4:8, NLT

You and I are designed for a continuous relationship with our
Creator. When we have that, we are in a state of completion.
This relationship leads us to a state where we are driven by
an intrinsic longing to live our life as God has intended. Our
state of being and our state of mind are significant.

I have found this passage from Philippians to be a guidepost
for my personal mental state. As the mental state is, so the
body will follow.

These thoughts of Paul lead us to characteristics of the Spirit,
such as the fruits of the Spirit outlined in Galatians 5:22–23,
NIV:

- Love
- Joy
- Peace
- Patience
- Kindness
- Goodness
- Gentleness

- Faithfulness
- Self-control

My hope is that this book is a resource for you to find your true connection in the midst of a difficult season. When it comes to your health, your focus can be drawn by seeking to overcome that which does not serve you. Instead, I encourage you to see this journey as an opportunity for God to do amazing work in you and, in turn, lead you to greater depth in your relationship with Him. God uses all things for His glory.

We are called to welcome that truth into our situations.

On your journey to receiving God's promise of complete healing, take one step at a time and find ways to feel encouraged and supported. Remain faithful along the way. Cultivate a daily practice, such as journaling or prayer time. Listen to and discern with God. Find your community and surround yourself with people who are supportive.

Execute research of healthcare coverage and types of medical professionals. Learn about various prescribed treatment programs. Research your own intervention. Put together a binder of your medical records and information you have discovered so they are all in one place. Create another binder for billing. Create a budget. Subscribe diligently to a plan that helps with the reality of payments.

Above all, remember God loves you, is with you, and is leading you. The journey is not straight. It is in His hands. We are to walk it along with Him. I would encourage you to recognize and maintain practices to help with self-reflection so you know when you are leaving God's path. Plug in my key components, such as love and grace.

Listen to those moments when things pop out at you or appear as recurring themes in your days. Do not deny these themes. Instead, digest them, listen to them, and bring them to your conversation with God.

Keep your focus on the relationship with Him and the rest will follow. He does what He does. Believe that it is true in your life as well.

I've shared many of the truths and tools God designed and brought me to understand in my life, and I pray that they will be of some service in yours as well. Thank you for your interest and know that you are never alone.

Next Steps

I am passionate about coming alongside those in need.

For more ways to connect, download free resources, and have further discussion, please come visit me on my Facebook page: NicoleMarie

You will find resources, such as:

- How to Discern
- How to Document (for self)
- How to Organize Healthcare Bills
- How to Choose the Right Medical Professional
- How to Prepare for the Appointment
- The Appointment Happened. Now What?
- Health Insurance Terms List
- Holy Spirit Recognition
- Discerning Self-Care
- How to Talk to Health Insurance Reps

You will also find these free resources:

- Calendar System
- Business Tasking System
- Medical Records Organization Template

Stop by my Facebook page and share how this book has impacted your journey. There you'll also find more information about me, such as blogs and speaking engagements.

Suggested Reading:

- *Switch On Your Brain,* by Dr. Caroline Leaf (Baker Books, 2013)

- *The Biology of Belief,* by Dr. Bruce Lipton (Hay House, 2008)

- *Success Is Not an Accident,* by Tommy Newberry (Tyndale, 2007)

- *Slight Edge,* by Jeff Olson [Greenleaf Book Group Press; 8 Anv edition (November 4, 2013)]

- *Let Your Life Speak,* by Parker Palmer (Jossey-Bass, 1999)

- *Life of the Beloved,* by Henri Nouwen (Crossroad, Anniversary Edition 2002)

- *Discernment,* by Henri Nouwen (HarperOne, 2013)

- *Restless,* by Jennie Allen (W Publishing, 2013)

- *The Energy Bus,* by Jon Gordon (Wiley, 2007)

- *The Practice of the Presence of God,* by Brother Lawrence (Whitaker House, 1982)

About the Author

I'm a child of God who is passionate about the power of God's love. Through life experience, I've come to understand how God is alive in our midst and how He longs for each of us to receive His gifts. My greatest joy is to share with others in the countless blessings this life has to offer.

In my free time, I enjoy exploring nature, watching goofy comedies, and taking walks with my husband, daughter, and our dog. I am passionate about empowering others to carve wholeness into their life, meaning walking alongside those who choose to live a life connected to mind, body, and spirit, enveloped in God's grace.

My love is to empower men and women through social media, public speaking, writing, or conversation.

I am humbly determined to live this life as a true gift from God. While I am grateful for the opportunities and countless blessings in my life, I attribute my greatest depth to the trials. The trials have been the birthplace of great growth in the spirit. This reality led to the birth of Relentless Healing and passion for all to experience all life has to offer—both the comfortable and the uncomfortable.

It is my hope that my ministry may be a guidepost for those seeking to further rely on God and to encourage and assist those seeking to weave God's glory into the very fabric of their being.

God is so faithful!